ACCLAIM

"At a time of extreme challenge for our nation's schools, *Bold School Principals* delivers extraordinary hope, in the form of rich, on-the-ground testimonies from successful school leaders. From inside classrooms, faculty meetings, parent gatherings, and more, the book brings the unmediated stories of school principals as they do the creative, complex work of fostering teacher leadership, supporting student learning and well-being, navigating antagonistic school cultures, and empowering and protecting staff. A unique and essential roadmap for school leadership."

Deanne Urmy, *Editor-at-large, Mariner Books*

"In this book, six principals give detailed, authentic, and wise self-portraits of their leadership journeys, providing helpful insights on the drama that plays out in every school and the strategies and tactics that make a positive difference for teaching and learning."

Kim Marshall, *Author: The Marshall Memo,*
former Boston Public Schools Teacher, Principal,
central office Curriculum Director

"At a time when the headlines are so full of stories about crises and failures in our schools, it is heartening to read such engaging accounts of how real leaders can drive positive change through vision, urgency, collaboration, persistence, and focus. These inspiring profiles of six outstanding leaders provide a range of models for all educators about what is realistically possible."

Douglas T. (Tim) Hall, *Morton H. and Charlotte Friedman*
Professor of Management Emeritus,
Boston University Questrom School of Business

"Bold School Principals takes the reader on a deep dive into the essence of school leadership. Applying keen insight and thorough research, it reveals numerous practical strategies that are based on essential values of six highly effective principals. This engaging book will help the reader learn how to motivate a school community and make critical moves that strengthen the school culture and lead to improved student learning."

David Castelline, *Executive Director at ELI,*
a division of Accept Collaborative

"This book is must reading for educators. Six school principals describe their growth and development in leading a school as a learning community. Through their mesmerizing stories, they demonstrate what I believe – that learning is the most fundamental human behavior. They provide individual and powerful examples of their own learnings: we all need to feel heard and valued; we all need to listen; we all need collaboration and communication to thrive."

Janet Whitla, *retired President and CEO,*
Education Development Center

"Artfully edited chapters give voice to creative principals bringing educational innovations to life in troubled schools. The authors highlight leadership principles, balanced and tailored to unique personalities and situations. This compelling book reveals schools as learning communities and leaders who use their hearts as well as their heads."

Martha Stone Wiske, *retired Lecturer and Researcher,*
Harvard Graduate School of Education

BOLD SCHOOL PRINCIPALS

Collaborative Practices
for Heightened Student Learning

GERALD C. LEADER WITH LOUISE LIPSITZ

PUBLISHER'S INFORMATION

ISBN: 978-1-953080-45-5

Author contact: gleader@bu.edu

Cover design by Kristin Leader

© 2023, Gerald C. Leader

ALL RIGHTS RESERVED

No part of this work covered by the copyright herein may be reproduced, transmitted, stored, or used in any form or by any means graphic, electronic, or mechanical, including but not limited to photocopying, scanning, digitizing, taping, Web distribution, information networks, or information storage and retrieval systems, except as permitted by Section 107 or 108 of the 1976 United States Copyright Act, without the prior written permission of the author.

EBookBakery Books

DEDICATION

To bold school principals everywhere who are making a profound, positive difference in the lives of learners, teachers, staff, and parents.

CONTENTS

INTRODUCTION

How does a school leader coalesce their faculty to achieve heightened student learning? Six experienced school leaders share their stories in their own words, in this book, *Bold School Principals: Collaborative Practices for Heightened Student Learning.* As leaders, they prioritized the school's strengths and needs. Ultimately, their goal was to develop trust with faculty that enabled everyone to solve issues that most impacted student learning.

Those who were new to their school, describe their entry planning; existing principals sought to evaluate what changes needed to be made. All six vigorously confronted the challenges required and made bold moves to create faculties as communities for increased student learning.

Each principal offered unique and diverse strategies, but common themes emerged across all six stories. It is the author's intent to engage readers in crafting their own solutions as school leaders.

As the founder and first director from 2002 to 2012 of the Educator Leadership Institute (ELI), a state licensed principal preparation and master's degree program, I chose to interview ELI graduates who were successful school leaders.

I selected four ELI graduates who stood out as exceptional educational leaders. Seeking a broader base for inclusion as case studies, I interviewed non-ELI graduates with excellent credentials as heads of schools and selected two. The entire group exemplified diversity in years of experience, racial background, gender, and in elementary, middle, and high school positions. Each principal was at their imaginative best as they crafted strategies utilizing their unique talents to coalesce their faculty.

I conducted multiple interviews, one-on-one, with each of the six candidates who had agreed to participate. My questions were open-ended so as not to bias their responses. "What has been the arc of your leadership career to date?" Some principals chose to start their narrative when they were a teacher, others when assuming the role as head of a school.

Each leader recalled their efforts to coalesce their faculty; moving their schools in new and innovative directions achieved from collaborative effort. The principals consciously crafted opportunities so that faculty could choose to engage in the change process.

The following six chapters each contain the edited interviews of each principal. A second portion of each chapter follows with authors' commentary focused on how the school leader coalesced their faculty to attain improved student learning. The conclusion of *Bold School Principals: Collaborative Practices for Heightened Student Learning* summarizes six common practices, across the leaders, that had substantial positive impact on each of their schools.

1

Eva Thompson

Oak Hill Middle School

2009-2013

Leadership Story

IN JUNE 2009, I became the Interim Principal at Oak Hill, one of four public middle schools in Newton, Massachusetts. The offer had been extended to me by Newton's Interim Superintendent of Schools and, with some trepidation, I accepted. Word within the district was that Oak Hill would be a tough nut to crack. The school had exhausted the repertoire of the previous principal who, with only one month's notice, had retired in June. Although I had been an elementary principal for 10 years and a middle school teacher for 6 years, I had no experience as a principal at the middle school level. After many years of teaching at several elementary schools and two middle schools, I had been invited as an interim candidate when the principalship became available. My 10 years record as an elementary principal was a strong one, which prompted the interim superintendent to seek me out for Oak Hill. Being the only remaining interested candidate for the position, I was intrigued by the culture and climate needs of the school and felt I could be of assistance. I embraced the challenge.

Entry

My entry started in July of 2009; it was essential for me to begin to build relationships and establish trust. As a result, I invited the entire staff, as well as four PTO (Parent Teacher Organization) representatives to come in and talk individually with me: I asked, "Tell me a bit about your journey. What led you to work at Oak Hill? What passions and interests fuel your work with students; how can I support you in your work?" I truly wanted to understand their hopes and dreams for the school and they responded with enthusiasm. Once school began in September, I joined students at their lunch tables just to chat and to hear about their experiences at the school. I visited classrooms daily and learned a lot about the relationships and instructional practices in place. I sought teachers out to inquire about their classes, their curriculum, their struggles and successes with students and families. Teachers became used to having me pop in for brief visits and were eager to share information about their teaching. Being visible to teachers and students was essential in forming relationships and establishing myself as a leader who cared about what was happening in the classrooms.

THE SCHOOL BUILDING

Small wins: When I arrived at Oak Hill, the building was in poor condition with regard to cleanliness and maintenance which influenced how people reacted to the school as a whole. When the senior custodian left at the end of my first year, I was able to hire custodians who really cleaned. It took two years to get the building to sparkle, and people saw the difference.

With PTO financial and manpower support, we revamped the teacher's room. It had been located downstairs and, due to its dungeon-like qualities, was rarely used. I moved it upstairs, and spent the summer of 2010 at IKEA decorating the room. I brought in new more comfortable chairs, and added a new user-friendly copy center in a refurbished storage area. When teachers returned in September of my second year, it was ready for them as a surprise and it looked awesome. The teachers' room became a meeting place for many teams and faculty members.

FAMILY ENGAGEMENT

In addition to becoming acquainted with faculty, staff, and students, I felt it important to engage the parent and family community in offering feedback about the school and to identify their wishes for the school under new leadership. In September 2009, at my suggestion the School Council distributed a survey to families. After compiling the findings, they shared themes with the parents. They identified *"The quality of the faculty"*, followed by *"quality of education, curriculum, and challenge"* as the two most positive aspects of Oak Hill. Where the school fell short was that there was almost no *"sense of community"* : families didn't feel connected to the school, or to teachers. They also reported that there were *"inconsistencies of practice, expectation, and experiences"* for their students from team to team; the quality of instruction varied.

To better meet the needs of families, I strategically involved the School Site Council, a parent and teacher leadership team, and the PTO leadership. Frequent communication with school community constituents helped make leadership decisions transparent. I kept teachers in the loop about these discussions through updates in my weekly notes. A biweekly newsletter to families detailed survey results and any plans to address the issues that surfaced.

One of the most well received new family engagement strategies was an outreach to families of incoming sixth graders. In the spring prior to their student's transition to Oak Hill, PTO leaders, guidance counselors, and I offered rising sixth grade families the opportunity to meet with us at their feeder elementary schools. Subsequently we would invite families to early morning coffees at Oak Hill that were coupled with student-led tours. Families loved hearing about the student experience first-hand, and asked the students questions they dared not ask adults. These initiatives were quite well received, and came to be highly anticipated community events.

ADMINISTRATIVE ASSISTANT STAFF

There was an undercurrent of discord among the school's four administrative assistants. It was readily addressed by bringing them together as a group to have open conversations regarding their individual needs for support, and to review their roles and responsibilities. We met a few more times throughout the year to check-in. One administrative assistant opted to retire at the end of the second year affording us the opportunity to hire someone new to join this team.

Existing Strengths/ Areas of Growth for Faculty

It was clear the teachers were passionate about teaching middle-school students. They appeared able to deliver quality instruction, but they were doing it in isolation. There was little if any communal synergy. I found it encouraging that some even wanted administrators in their classes, observing and coaching, and offering supportive feedback.

However, a major take away from my entry interviews with faculty was that Oak Hill was a severely fractured community. Faculty members talked of cliques of teachers that didn't interact with each other. People would walk by each other in the hall without offering a greeting; they didn't know each other. There was finger pointing, "this group does this", or "this group does that". Small groups were friendly with one another but these friendly relationships often did not cross teams or grade levels. Lack of fairness in teaching assignments and class size contributed to divisions among faculty. There was a lack of clarity regarding how and why these decisions were made. There was little vertical or horizontal alignment of the curriculum.

Assessment of student progress was an issue. Student performance was based upon lesson/unit test scores: "autopsies" at year's end versus using common formative assessments to monitor growth and adjust instruction as units were taught. Teachers at a grade level teaching the same content area operated independently so common planning, common student-centered goals and common performance assessments were atypical, occurring in just a few places. Teaching for coverage was more the focus than teaching for true understanding. There was a need for support structures for those struggling students who did not have identified special needs. Faculty meetings were scary places to be for some teachers. Teachers reported that it wasn't uncommon for people to attack each other without being called on to change their behavior. Giving a presentation was a risk; people feared being verbally abused. Many people gave up contributing to faculty meetings all together.

The whole student's needs were not an instructional focus. Understanding students' social-emotional needs and recognizing the efficacy of student engagement strategies were not pervasive systematic practices despite good intentions. Instead, homework completion, behavior compliance and test scores dominated many teachers' mindsets. Student behavior in the cafeteria was out of control and disrespectful to teachers. There were no systems in place to address behavior at the school. Discipline was perceived to be handled differently by the two.

ASSISTANT PRINCIPALS

Parents were kept at bay. They were seen as too demanding and unrealistic in their expectations . From teachers' perspective, parents felt unwelcome in the school because administrators had signaled to them that "middle-school students need their independence". There was also fear and skepticism about why I was chosen to lead Oak Hill

FACULTY, PARENT AND STUDENT SURVEYS: STAKEHOLDER INPUT

To create a comprehensive picture of the state of the school:

• In September of my first year, I administered a teacher and staff survey. The findings were consistent with what I had learned through my previous entry interviews. They assessed themselves as highly skilled and competent, and felt blessed with "great" students, but felt there was a lack of faculty cohesion. They saw themselves in isolation with no sharing among peers.

• With the School Council, we administered a parent survey and designed a response plan to share back thematic results and next steps.

• I gathered informal feedback from students as I held lunchroom chats with them in the early fall.

Compiling and interpreting survey results took time. I prepared a slide presentation for parents and teachers to share with what I learned through my entry process. These presentations occurred in February-March. Throughout the fall and early winter, rather than highlighting and labeling the interpersonal negative climate issues too early, I used the time to actively engage staff during faculty meeting time and in grade level and team meetings in getting to know and working with one another. We focused on aspects of collaborative functioning, teaming and how we communicate with one another when differences arose. Having tightly facilitated meetings was a change in itself.

I believed the Oak Hill faculty wanted to change but didn't know what or how to change. My goal for Oak Hill was to help teachers understand how to collaborate effectively and inspire them to intentionally learn with and from one another. Oak Hill's student performance scores were in the proficient range for most students, but not those in special education or for students of color. My look at the underlying instructional process at Oak Hill suggested sustained improvement was not necessarily assured. I felt faculty couldn't focus on issues of student achievement or engagement until we were able to function as a more collaborative organization of adults with clear articulated goals. We desperately needed to improve team functioning within the school, and that became the priority my first year. I was well aware that functioning in teams did not come naturally to everyone; it was a skill that needed to be taught and honed to build the capacity of the group. I have long believed that fostering teacher leadership builds capacity for individuals as well as the larger group. Teachers learn best with and from one another.

FIRST FACULTY GATHERING: LAYING THE GROUNDWORK FOR COLLABORATION

In my entry conversations I learned that some people did not feel psychologically safe in faculty meetings where airtime was often dominated by a "vocal minority". My emphasis and mantra for the year, repeated over and over again, was: *One, we learn with and from one another to support student learning* and to emphasize our strength as a faculty – *two, we care deeply about students, their learning, and well-being*. Given these two premises, at the first full faculty gathering of the year I wanted to set the stage for how we were going to learn together to create an Oak Hill community that gave priority to student learning and included everyone's development. The structure of the faculty gathering would follow a clear agenda and a consistent meeting format to optimize participant learning and would launch the same format for all subsequent professional learning activities versus traditional business-focused faculty meetings.

• A written agenda, with explicit statements of anticipated learning outcomes and meeting norms posted on the reverse side for easy reference.

• Essential roles assigned to faculty: Facilitator, Observer, Timekeeper. The 'Observer to Norms' role was solicited in advance with people selected who were most comfortable modeling and offering feedback to the group.

• A brief icebreaker or warm-up activity to help teachers learn about one another.

• Opportunity for working in small and/or large groups with a variety of teachers across departments depending on the nature of tasks.

• Feedback collected after each faculty gathering using a feedback survey seeking lessons learned and areas for further development. These became known as "Tickets to Leave" and were intended to complete the learning loop for every professional learning activity.

I gave careful thought to the physical organization of the meeting space, including where people would be seated to ensure that they got to know one another better. Teachers were accustomed to coming to faculty meetings and sitting wherever they wanted thus reinforcing existing isolated groups, and the new structure stopped that. At every faculty meeting which were professional learning opportunities, I arranged seating in small groups, sometimes randomly and other times intentionally connecting people who did not routinely come in contact with one another.

My opening day presentation emphasized exploring, sharing, and learning together in response to these questions: "What does it mean to be collaborative vs. congenial? How can collaborative functioning impact student achievement? How and when do we use assessment as part of the teacher learning process, and for what purpose?"

I explained my role as principal was to "hit the ground listening", ask curious questions to learn, and to create the systems and structures to support teachers and staff to do their best. My welcome message recognized their desire to work as a cohesive community and that we were going to work toward that goal together. I endorsed Oak Hill's existing Mission Statement: Ensuring that all students achieve.

I also recognized that our first gathering couldn't be passive: with faculty listening as I did all the talking. If a collaborative community was the aspiration, teachers needed to talk and most importantly, with each other. They needed to know each other. To that end, we used a "get to know you" experiential exercise to start the meeting. The faculty was divided into four groups, including membership spanning the youngest to the most veteran faculty members. In the foursome, each introduced themselves by name, role, and number of years at Oak Hill. Then each person had one minute to share at least one hope and one fear for the coming academic year. It was fascinating to watch teachers interact in creative non-verbal ways. There was some pride for those who had been in the school the longest, a nod to veteran teachers. After thanking folks for their participation, we moved on to our focus for the year.

I introduced the five key questions for collaborative learning communities, which Newton middle school principals had adapted from the book, *The Collaborative Teacher*, 2008, by Erkens et al. They would become Oak Hill's guiding focus over the next four years. By responding to the questions, teams would redirect their attention away from what they taught and towards the impact of their instruction on student achievement.

1. What is it we expect our students to learn?

2. How will we teach it so that all students can learn it?

3. How will we know when they have learned it?

4. How will we respond when they don't learn?

5. How will we respond when they already know it?

I was completely committed to shared leadership. The faculty and staff responsibilities were to serve students and parents; while the administrative team and I were responsible for serving the needs of teachers. I could only do my job if I was working collaboratively in concert with teachers. Only then could we reap the benefits of learning from one another, sharing and listening to ideas to forge our next steps.   .

Making the Case for Collaboration: Shifting School Culture through Professional Learning

The opening gathering was not complete until the faculty engaged in the exercise "Are we a GROUP or a TEAM". Teachers were organized into five-person groups to experience the increased performance outcomes of a problem-solving exercise when they collaborated compared with when they tackled the same exercise individually. When participants reflected on why collaboration had better outcomes, their comments included: "We shared strategies"; "We divided the task and shared responsibility"; "We used the data from previous rounds to determine strengths and create our plan for improvement". In this activity, we were laying the groundwork for working in teams with a common shared purpose.

Apart from classroom instruction, every available time within the contractual week would be spent on professional development activities. I'd handle administrative tasks outside school hours, and communicate through my Weekly Notes newsletter made available each Sunday night. It shared important information for the week and key updates on school matters. Understanding that teachers had limited time available, email communication was restricted to unexpected news to keep the focus on the Notes as a primary communication vehicle. Tuesday afternoons had previously been set aside for department meetings. We modified those gatherings, creating professional development opportunities.

As a district, Newton's middle school professional development priority was collaboration. *The Collaborative Teacher: Working Together as a Professional Learning Community* by Erkens and Jakicic became a required read for all faculty. Chapter by chapter, month by month, we disaggregated the lessons and applied them to Oak Hill. Part of the District's effort was a new memorandum of agreement between the Teacher's Association (the Union) and the District. The memorandum defined workload expectations and determined the frequency of meetings at the grade, department and team levels, and supported having time to collaborate with one another.

Building Teacher Leadership: Empowering an Instructional Leadership Team

The District created the "Content Facilitators" position, teacher leadership roles, which drew from faculty at each school to serve as links between school-based curriculum departments and the District curriculum co cordinators. The new position provided the perfect opportunity for me to form the Facilitators into an Instructional Leadership Team. In addition to serving as liaisons, the Content Facilitator group was a great sounding board for me in terms of my decision making. A firm believer in the power of distributed leadership, I also valued their input in helping shape professional development meetings. They served two-year terms, with staggered rotation, a mix of veterans and newer members.

Along with everyone, I benefited tremendously from this team's good thinking. They clearly recognized how to appeal to their colleagues from their knowledge base and used good humor effectively. While the team gained confidence in their planning, initially they doubted their ability to facilitate meetings in their departments; folks were intimidated. Before our next professional development meeting I wrote up and distributed a cheat sheet with facilitation guidelines. It was essentially a step-by-step guide on facilitation including tips on how to manage resistance.

Teachers were to first meet in small mixed groups to debrief The Collaborative Teacher's Chapter 2 – *"Creating Intentional Collaboration"* with assigned roles for facilitator, timekeeper, note taker, and observer to norms. It was highly structured and focused. The Facilitators led their departments in conversations about their "current reality" and next steps for team functioning.

In hindsight, I realized that the Facilitators could have used more practice implementing these strategies. Facilitators were met with mixed success. I circulated among some of the "needier" department groups, where some teachers reverted to old behaviors, treating the meeting as an opportunity to raise concerns about managerial issues such as ordering supplies or general griping. I hadn't thoroughly prepared the Content Facilitators for gently but firmly guiding people back to the task at hand. I also did not clearly articulate that the expectations of this meeting differed from previous meetings. For me, this was just a first attempt.

We learned from the experience; and subsequent facilitation would need more modeling and practice in order to be met with greater success. Managing adaptive challenges were not part of the Facilitators' existing skills. Despite missteps, Facilitators were willing to give it another try.

Administrative Team

In the early months I became increasingly aware that my job was to enhance the leadership capacity of the assistant principals. I needed to work through them to reach teachers and the school. They needed to be empowered as leaders, which meant we had to consistently be on the same page in our approaches with the greater community. We ourselves needed to coalesce as a team.

My vision of our purpose as a team was to support teachers, students, and families. We also needed to be confidential support for one another. We valued and relied on our norms: being open and offering forthright feedback; being conscious of how concerns are put on the table; supporting each other's growth; assuming positive intentions; being willing to share vulnerabilities and supporting the vulnerabilities of others.

We dubbed our Administrative Team the 'A' Team. We met weekly on Mondays; the time slot was held sacred. Each meeting opened with the sharing of "small successes" from the previous week. We thoughtfully created norms for how we would function together and how we could hold each other accountable for assigned tasks. We rotated roles of team facilitation, notetaker, observer of this team and met in the corresponding facilitator's office.

Putting Collaboration into Practice Across the School

For the sake of my credibility and the school's progress as a community, I needed to model a number of things: how meeting time could be used effectively, how we could learn professionally '*with*' and '*from*' each other, how to ensure a safe working climate, how to engage teachers' thinking as input, and how to celebrate success along the way. I modeled needed structures: a clear agenda with anticipated meeting outcomes, agreed upon norms, and clear roles for participants. Meetings needed to begin and end on time. Meeting content needed to reflect teacher needs and be planned based on their input through the Content Facilitators. Meetings included a lot of small group work to foster relationship building, increase engagement, and stimulate reflection on current work as well as next steps. My faculty meetings often mirrored the elements of a sound instructional lesson: an icebreaker or warm up to anchor learning by accessing prior knowledge; a task that added new content or skills; a task to apply or do something with new content or skills during the meeting; an "away" task that connected the new learning back to a plan for next steps, and a ticket to leave as a feedback loop for facilitators.

ACTIVE LISTENING AND CANDID ACKNOWLEDGMENT OF FACULTY PERSPECTIVES

I repeatedly heard people mention with derision, all the school initiatives that had come and gone. "Initiative fatigue" was at play, with state and district initiatives coming top-down, and the school still dealing with the aftermath of unsuccessful initiatives led by the previous principals. The faculty wondered if my emphasis on collaboration was just another expectation for them to tolerate before it disappeared. I acknowledged their justifiable frustration and empathized with them by providing an opportunity to publicly and safely share their emotions. My hope was that we could move forward with meaningful conversations about collaboration. In response I devised an activity focused on doing just that. I created a five by three foot long negative to positive continuum chart and placed it at the front of the room. I asked teachers to jot down previous initiatives on sticky notes, then place them on the chart along the continuum assigning them positive/negative value for professional learning and impact on student achievement. We then debriefed: "Why did you place each initiative where you did on the continuum?" "What practice was still in place?" "What are our key takeaways?"

Teachers had a great time unloading their angst and sharing common experiences while also acknowledging their more positive ones. I connected the activity back to our current focus on collaborating as a way of operating focused on learning together, versus being an activity that comes and goes. As a takeaway for our ongoing planning, I asked everyone to respond to the "Ticket to Leave" prompt: *What's one initiative that you'd like to see carried forward?* Responses varied, yet a common theme emerged: they enjoyed the opportunity to work with colleagues on interdisciplinary work.

Year one was devoted to team cohesion and adjusting systems that weren't functioning well for teachers or students. We began consistently enforcing cafeteria rules and coverage, balancing student assignment and teacher workloads, and supporting teacher collaboration with a focus on student achievement. We also began to consider what effective instruction looked like and how to draw teacher attention to monitoring student engagement, two areas I noticed as needing attention in my walkthroughs.

ORGANIZATIONAL STRUCTURES AND SYSTEMS: MODELING TRANSPARENCY AND CONSISTENCY

One of my goals was to ensure that clear and consistently enacted systems and structures for communication and functioning were in place for all school groups. This included putting them in writing so they could be referenced by anyone at any time. Having them in writing also helped cement the message. Each constituent group in the school (the Content Facilitator Team, Administrative Team, etc.) had regularly scheduled meetings with assigned roles for the facilitator and note-taker. We designed a consistent meeting structure with agreed upon norms, and clarity about our function and purpose that was continually revisited.

COMMUNICATION: POSITIVE ALTERNATIVES TO POLARIZING LANGUAGE

In November 2009, I received permission from the district to hire a consultant to work with us on being aware of the language we used to ensure it respected different perspectives. It was common to hear people speak about students, families and one another in subjective terms that came across as labels. "Student A was a *bad* student." "Colleague X would *never* acknowledge others in the hallway." "This mother is *always* difficult." "'Student B *never* raises his hand." This polarizing language didn't support collaborative interactions, even when used unintentionally. The two consultants led us in two interactive sessions that considered positive language alternatives: "and vs but", reframing use of labels, etc., the power of impact vs. intent, and identifying how different groups within the school were perceived. In addition to key takeaways we asked teachers to provide positive and constructive feedback. The results were powerful in that teachers were very clear about what did and didn't work for them. Teachers recognized the need to consider various perspectives, the needs of others, the power of impact and intent, and ways to adjust use of language.

APPRECIATING WORK STYLES

A key stepping stone along our path to becoming a collaborative community was to understand each other's work styles and perspectives. It seemed to me that many people held fossilized views of one another. I truly believed they would benefit from understanding what motivates people to act the way they do. I hoped that many would recognize we all perceived the world and our interactions through varied lenses. Rather than assign negative attributes to people, I wanted them to recognize style similarities, differences and needs. I invited a Central Office curriculum person to lead this session so I could participate alongside the teachers. We asked teachers which one of four Compass Point "directions" most closely described their personal style?

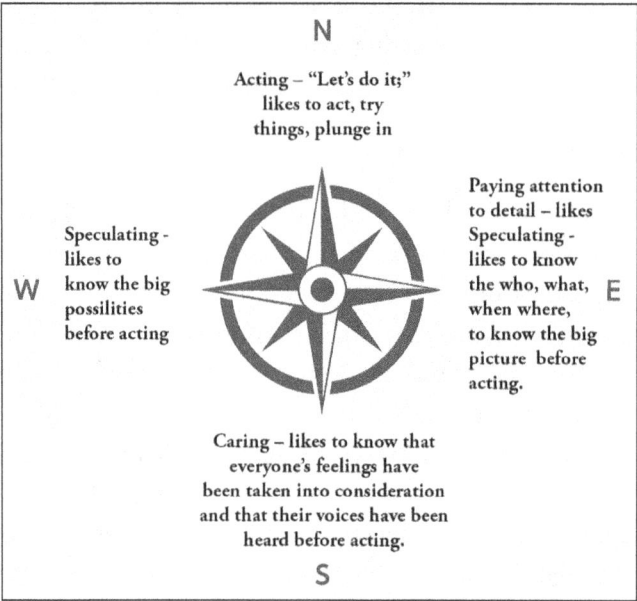

N

Acting – "Let's do it;"
likes to act, try
things, plunge in

Paying attention
to detail – likes
Speculating -
likes to know
the who, what,
when where,
to know the big
picture before
acting.

E

Speculating -
likes to
know the big
possibilities
before acting

W

Caring – likes to know that
everyone's feelings have
been taken into consideration
and that their voices have been
heard before acting.

S

Adapted from *The Personality Compass: A New Way to Understand People* by Diane Turner and Thelma Greco, 1998

Teachers were then directed to assemble in four groups based on their self-selected work style preference to consider the following prompts:

- What are the strengths of your style? (4 adjectives)
- What are the limitations of your style? (4 adjectives)
- What style do you find most difficult to work with and why?
- What do people from the other "directions" or work styles need to know about you so you can work together effectively?
- What do you value about the other three styles?

To wrap up the session, each group shared their major takeaways. I believe the task was a success because it was interactive, fun, non- threatening due to the group structure, along with the effectiveness of the facilitator –there was limited pushback beyond the anticipated hesitation of selecting just one style for the purposes of the exercise.

In subsequent communications, I referenced the importance of considering learning style preferences when embarking on any group work. As an example, I asked the Facilitators to guess which was my preferred compass point. Several were accurate in identifying me as a combination of East and West. This afforded me the opportunity to share that I depended on others who brought North and South tendencies to interactions and decision-making. The Content Facilitators then tried to identify one another's styles. By April, we felt safe enough that this was a low-risk conversation and we appreciated hearing each other's thoughts, perceptions and rationales for leaning towards one style or another.

SCHOOL IMPROVEMENT PLAN:

In April 2010, the state-mandated need for a School Improvement Plan became a school-wide agenda item. We were tasked with developing a specific action plan to improve student learning that built upon the change efforts already underway. Oak Hill's school improvement planning record to date had been minimal at best, with little faculty involvement.

As a newbie I could have followed a similar course of inaction for the following year. But doing so would have denied the faculty the opportunity to practice their newly developed collaborative skills while continuing their ownership of Oak Hill's mission. We asked them to identify two or three areas that needed work at the school. My invitation was greeted with enthusiasm and their responses exhibited genuine thoughtfulness. It was clear they wanted to be involved in the development of the School Improvement Plan that could make a difference in how we operated and served students.

After reviewing the feedback, we came up with five different areas that translated into our Study Group work for the following year: 1) Instructional Practices, 2) Response to Intervention (RTI), 3) Behavioral Expectations, 4) Student Connections, 5) School Spirit: Fun and Vibrant Team. Teachers enjoyed having choice in their professional learning and liked working in cross-disciplinary groups. Our plan was to have the teachers self-select which group they wanted to join for a year-long study starting that May.

Teachers selected their group and I was gratified with the diversity of outlooks represented within each group. I was pleased the Compass Points activity as well as other interactive structures proved to be a prompt, which primed teachers for working with a highly diverse group of colleagues. The Study Groups would put their collaboration training to the test. I assigned the three assistant principals as facilitators to groups. A fourth group was facilitated by my Administrative Intern, a teacher at the school, and I led the fifth group: Instructional Practices.

The Study Groups gave the faculty the opportunity to set Oak Hill's direction, and they were eager to take on the challenge. The following year, 2010-11, the majority of our faculty meeting time was spent working in our Study Groups. We developed a number of Study Group Guidelines to keep structural consistency across groups. For example, groups were to be self-directed, co-chaired by an administrator or teacher. Also meeting notes were to be recorded and shared in an online folder, so that faculty members could provide feedback. Study Groups were encouraged to research and identify best practices related to their group's topic.

I told the faculty they were going to create and execute a plan to improve student learning at Oak Hill. I encouraged the use of an Action Research process: First: taking stock of the current reality, and using evidence to show how we currently function. Step two was to research what other schools are doing, and what are the best practices in the focus area. This involved consulting middle school journals and other schools' websites for ideas. Third: organize the evidence. Step four included analysis of the information and create an action plan, including ways to determine the potential impact on student learning. Then finally, to plan next steps based on the results of the process.

Planning for Faculty Study Groups Year Two - Four: Embedded Collaborative Teamwork

In the first Study Group session in May, I brought everyone's attention back to the year's focus on collaborative work. The common agenda included the following *must-do processes:*

- Review process, select roles

- Appoint an "Observer" who would provide supportive feedback to the group

- Refer to Norms & Guidelines for Communication,

- Keep it positive, move forward: no blame, no shame,

- Connect to "Compass" points – we approach ideas, tasks from different perspectives,

- Build on prior work: collaboration, 'language we use,'

- Keep focus on student achievement, student needs.

The Instructional Practices Study Group divided into three subgroups: homework, peer visits, and checking for understanding, which I focused on. Another Group called themselves the "Fun and Vibrant" group; they were all about school and faculty spirit. These included those who cared deeply about making connections, having fun, and being active. I was glad there were people interested because this was not my forte or primary interest. You hear people in every middle school complaining about how student behavior is handled, so our "Behavioral Expectations" group focused on that. Another group was "Response to Intervention": composed mostly of Special Education and Guidance staff. Finally, there was a "Caring Community Group" focusing on how we foster a caring community of adults and students.

I had high expectations for the Study Groups and wasn't disappointed. However, the "Behavioral Expectations" group needed rescuing. It was unclear whether the problem was the leadership, the membership or a combination of both. Coming to philosophical agreement wasn't part of their repertoire. My Administrative Intern was leading it, and had to work extremely hard just to keep the group on an even keel. Prickly personalities were a real problem. I would sit in occasionally just to make myself visible, but quite frankly I'm not sure my presence did much good. I was hoping they could get to a place where they were able to address some school-wide behavior issues, but they couldn't agree on the foundation needed to work together: approaches or consistency in interacting with one another.

INSTRUCTIONAL PRACTICES STUDY GROUP

Teachers were absorbed in teaching versus being focused on impact on student learning. I wanted to be sure teachers were aware of their impact on students' thoughts and reflections. That next year, we introduced lots of ways to check for understanding and ensure student engagement.

For the Peer Visits group, we started by randomly pairing teachers up, and sent them on treasure hunts - exploring each other's classrooms to find some instructional treasure in the room whether something they saw on the wall or something that they saw kids doing or something that made the lesson special. Everybody in the school went on walks, and described their treasure on a piece of paper. They stood up and read them at faculty meetings. Then we posted them in the teachers' room so that people could read them when they were photocopying. It was very affirming. Faculty members loved it.

This was followed by "Learning Walks". I structured peer visits to be low level, low stress, and low risk. My leadership team and I created a quasi-instructional rounds protocol, facilitating teachers going into each other's classrooms and focusing on what kids are saying and doing. I showed them how to capture this observational data without making judgments. The protocol started the process of making both teachers' and students' thinking visible.

We engaged in Learning Walks again the next year. Teachers were so eager to learn from each other by being in each other's classrooms. It was exciting for them to realize how much they took away from these visits. To optimize these learnings we set up mini workshop sessions where teachers had an opportunity to visit three different teachers who had had presentations on a particularly effective instructional practice that they had created in their classroom.

Collaboration for me, is all about learning from one another then helping students learn. This protocol was so effective that we institutionalized the process so it could be replicated in other middle schools.

CARING COMMUNITY STUDY GROUP

Caring Community was all about student connections, how students made connections with adults and with one another. I wasn't alone in feeling that the Community block structure (a quasi-advisory structure) in place when I started was too loosey-goosey. It was essentially two teachers meeting with 25 kids once a month. A number of teachers also felt the community block of time wasn't being used effectively. Kids weren't really forming relationships with adults or each other in ways that would make them feel welcome at the school. I knew they were having a good time, but it was difficult to track whether a real impact was being made. The members of the Caring Community group were well meaning, but they couldn't decide on anything. I really had to blow up the group and start over because they were not making progress with meaningful revisions. I got some money from the District to work in the summer; that attracted a group of faculty who were really passionate about creating a Caring Community with a focused sensible plan. They were quite effective!

They put together a program that was admirable. Every faculty member became an advisor to 10 kids, and every Friday morning for half an hour they met with their kids. Everybody in the school followed the same structure for the same amount of time. There was always an opening greeting, then, some kind of sharing activity, which the kids generated. These structures were drawn from Responsive Classroom practices. There were always goals that could be measured in pre- and post-surveys.

I was the only one in the building that didn't have a ten-student group. The Caring Community Study Group wanted one person who would be able to hold people accountable for what they were supposed to be doing. I would go on a visit, see what they were doing, and offer feedback as needed. We added a number of embellishments, such as having people submit their 'recipes for success' for effective activities to implement during Community and these were shared with the faculty.

Fun and Vibrant Study Group

A group of teachers stepped up to enliven the school community. They instituted First Friday breakfast for faculty and everybody brought breakfast for the whole faculty before school. First Fridays continued on a monthly basis. They also instituted monthly themed school spirit days. One theme was having everyone dress up as their favorite character. There were basketball games between students and teachers during March Madness; the whole school got involved and it was a lot of fun. Teachers did fun, silly things and dressed up like clowns and cheerleaders at the games. I joined as a cheerleader. At first glance, the Fun and Vibrant Group felt light and fluffy to me yet I realized that school spirit activities fuel some people. That's not really where I put my energy, so I was glad other people in the building had this interest. This group was successfully dedicated to fostering this positive energy.

AFFIRMATION AT THE FINAL FACULTY MEETING OF THE YEAR.

On the last day of school for faculty in 2010, I shared some reflections on our successes and areas for continued improvement as a school. I then asked teachers to reflect on their work and to share, in groups of four, their thoughts on:

1. One instructional strategy that worked well this year.

2. One thing that you did differently this year that you'll continue next year.

After thanking people for their work, one teacher rose and announced that I needed to be acknowledged for all my hard work that year. That's when everyone stood up and began to applaud. I was surprised, pleased that my efforts were recognized, and a bit embarrassed to be the focus of so much attention. I firmly believed we were moving forward as a community in more productive ways and the spontaneous display affirmed for me that I had much of the group on my side and they were willing to move forward, rather than stand still or go backwards. When invited to offer their feedback on any of our undertakings, the group was honest and largely helpful in offering potential next steps. My job was to continue to genuinely solicit input and make decisions with their participation. We all knew that we did not always agree, yet there was a commonly held belief that I was fair and supportive of the teachers.

Summarizing the work over my four year tenure in the school, there are throughlines as the work either continued or extended from the previous year's work - demonstrating the teachers' request for no new disconnected initiatives! By year four, we were solidly implementing and solidifying instructional skills and programmatic practices. The district rolled out a revamped model for Supervision and Evaluation of Teachers using a rubric adapted from Massachusetts Department of Elementary and Secondary Education. We integrated that work with our goal setting and Professional Learning Community work which was structured in Grade Level Department Teams. There we had also begun to create formative assessments to monitor student progress. Not everyone was convinced these were important so clearly further work was needed for teachers to understand their validity and need.

Throughout this time, our MCAS (Massachusetts state benchmark tests) scores improved particularly for students receiving special education; and the gap was narrowed for students of color. We were carefully tracking student growth percentiles (year-over-year score comparisons for individual students) as these helped us hone in on particular students in need. In year four, we designed a unique intervention support program for grades 7 and 8 in math and ELA; and grade 6 students received support from the literacy coach. A version of that intervention structure exists today, over a decade later.

The "Community" block has been revamped to become an Advisory block at all four middle schools across the district with a clear focus on the social-emotional needs of students, especially given the pandemic. *Making Thinking Visible* continues to be utilized as a resource for teaching and learning. There was much work to be celebrated when I left at the end of four years: the school culture and climate had a restart, faculty relations became less divided and the need for collaborative teaming was more fully embraced. A good number of the faculty remain and continue to be energized by middle school students!

Eva's early exhaustive information gathering on the state of the school as she entered Oak Hill provided her with an opportunity to begin the process of establishing a mutually respectful relationship with each faculty member, a significant priority for her in her leadership practice.

From the start of her tenure at Oak Hill, she was focused on coalescing a collaborative community so that they learned with and from each other to advance student learning. Observing a faculty that worked alongside one another without acknowledging the power of collaboration and practicing it, Eva set her sights on moving her team of teachers forward through carefully planned training exercises and self-discovery.

Oak Hill had high promise just below the surface of an antagonistic school climate. Competent faculty enjoyed teaching middle-schoolers but they did it with little or no assistance from each other, mitigating the potential of synergistic outcomes. The decisiveness of Eva's diagnosis, that Oak Hill suffered from an absence of collaborative skills and the intentionality of her remedial plan, suggested she had encountered and dealt with a similar issue in a previous school venue. Eva's change plan to coalesce the community for higher student learning was built on the process of faculty learning and practicing collaborative skills. Eva laid the groundwork for collaborative teaming through employing a series of carefully planned professional learning experiences where Eva enabled the faculty to recognize and practice collaborative teaming, learning with and from each other rather than collegial "group" work.

The final section of Eva's collaboration preparation effort gave the faculty the opportunity to participate in and influence the course of Oak Hill as a school. Given the autonomy to choose and prioritize the most critical problems facing Oak Hill, the faculty engaged in whole school change initiatives and committed to implementing their selected action steps. Through her explicit professional development modeling the value of working as a team, Eva created the structure, consistency and emotional safety needed for faculty to become vulnerable with one another. Her thoughtful planning shifted faculty interactions from collegial groups to collaborative teams and provided opportunities for the faculty to learn together. Eva delegated responsibility for school improvement to them, thereby coalescing her faculty. In their self-selected study groups, faculty members took on leadership roles and focused their attention on their ultimate goal: improved student learning.

2

MATT STAHL

PAWTUCKETVILLE ELEMENTARY SCHOOL

2010-2015

DR. AN WANG MIDDLE SCHOOL

2015-present

LEADERSHIP STORY

DOUGLAS ADAMS WROTE, "I may not have gone where I intended to go, but I think I have ended up where I needed to be," which sums up my journey into the world of school leadership. I got my business management degree and worked in the art museum world for a few years before becoming an urban educator and principal at both elementary and middle school levels. After eight years of teaching in the Boston Public Schools district, I yearned to become a principal because I felt like I could have a bigger impact, make a bigger change. The Educator Leadership Institute (ELI) program allowed me to get my principal's license without sacrificing a full-time salary, which essentially made it possible to get the license without putting my family's financial security at risk. Enrolling in the ELI program was my first step toward school leadership. I hadn't intended to become a school leader, but it was exactly where I was supposed to be in my life.

THE WASHINGTON SCHOOL

After finishing ELI, I spent a year and a half interviewing for principalship positions all over Massachusetts. I ended up throwing my name into the ring for principalship of a large-scale public elementary school in Lowell. When I got a call for an interview, the superintendent explained that I might be a better fit for the Washington School, another elementary school in the district. Although It was much smaller, it was a well-established school with a student-centered culture. If hired, I would be taking over from an excellent principal who was retiring. It was a safe place for the superintendent to take a chance on hiring a new principal.

Looking back on that conversation now, her recommendation makes complete sense. I'd never been a principal and was an unknown quantity. Without question, the largest growth in my career took place during my first few years as a brand-new principal at the Washington School. The outgoing principal helped me get my feet on the ground and provided guidance on what it meant to be a principal. She showed me the ropes—how she had run things and how the school worked. The responsibilities of a principal were very different from that of a teacher, and I had to learn how I needed to carry myself as the instructional leader of a building. All of a sudden, I was dealing primarily with adults, which required a very different skill set than teaching students.

During those formative years at Washington School, I found my administrative voice. I didn't have an assistant principal because it was such a small school, but I was lucky enough to have an amazing social worker. She was the only other administrator in the building. Our personalities were on opposite ends of the spectrum; she taught me a lot about tempering myself as the leader of the building. By nature, I shoot from the hip—I say things without a lot of filtering. Although admittedly to this day, I still don't have much of a filter between my brain and what comes out of my mouth, I have learned that sometimes taking a step back before speaking is essential.

Being a leader doesn't mean that you have all the answers. It entails creating an effective, collaborative coalition of people who get the work done on a daily basis at the school. Over those first three years at Washington School, I learned that being a leader meant getting everyone in the building involved. Even though you've got good ideas and you feel like you're doing the right thing, getting others to follow your vision is just as important.

FINDING MY ADMINISTRATIVE VOICE

I didn't always have to be the typical formal kind of principal at the Washington School. The faculty was very tight-knit and they were excited to have a renewed sense of excitement coming from the principal's office. My leadership style was not as "polished" as other principals, but because the faculty already functioned effectively as a team, I was able to be less formal than most first-time principals. On the one hand, a teacher could scream across the hallway, "Hey Matt—I need you, get in here!" and that was perfectly fine. On the other hand, the teachers looking for a more traditional approach would say, "Mr. Stahl, could I make an appointment with you to talk about some things?" and that was fine, too. It was a great opportunity for me to develop my own "voice" and experiment with it as a leader. Because the school was so well established, I could take some chances without risking the school falling apart.

As a principal, you've got to figure out how to work with all different adults—both faculty members and parents. While on some level, they have to adjust to your style when you take over a school, there is no question that you have to also adjust your style to them. In those first couple of years, that's where I learned I can't always just be "me," be Matt. There were times where I had to be "Mr. Stahl." Part of my role as a leader was to figure out what each person needed from me in a given situation: do they need Mr. Stahl, Matt, or someone in between?

I was at the Washington School for five years, essentially as a lone administrator. I was fairly successful in keeping the momentum of the previous principal, and we continued to have academic growth each and every year. Our state testing scores increased annually during my administrative journey, and the school was eventually identified as a Level 1 school—the highest possible designation for a school in Massachusetts.

FROM PRINCIPAL TO "FIREMAN"

During my third year at the Washington School, the state was struggling with significant budget issues. The district made the tough decision to cut the principalship position at the Moody Elementary School, another small elementary school in Lowell. I was asked to become principal of both schools, still without an assistant principal. Logistically it was a tough shift; Moody was on the other side of the city. In addition, the superintendent assigned me without consulting with their faculty, who had been hoping for an internal promotion. Much like Washington School, Moody was a very family-based school and there was a strong, tight-knit faculty in the building. Although they hadn't had the level of success that the Washington School had over the years, they were still a very stable school community. As the "assigned" principal, it was hard to break into that community. I had to learn a whole new set of delegation skills. I had to make sure I had strong teacher leaders in both buildings. I wanted to ensure there were people to rely on when there was an emergency and I was outside the building.

The plan for the following year was for me to move from Washington and Moody to another elementary school in the district. The original idea was a swap between myself and the principal at Pawtucketville Elementary School, a larger school with around 600 students. The superintendent wanted to insert a powerful voice there—introduce someone who could shake things up. Pawtucketville was designated a Level 4 school by the state, which was the second-lowest designation in Massachusetts at the time. A Level 5 designation indicated a state takeover of the building. At this point, I was ready for the new challenge of a larger school. Life rarely works out the way you expect, however, and the principal who I was supposed to be swapping with retired out of the blue.

Instead of hiring another principal, the superintendent made the decision to have me supervise all three elementary schools at the same time. My job description that year went from handling a school with about 600 students and 60 staff members (Pawtucketville) to a situation where I would be dealing with 1,100 students and over 120 staff members at three different buildings spread out across the city.

That was the most challenging professional year I've had in my entire career. It was a huge learning experience for me because I had no choice but to learn how to prioritize situations at each of the schools. On any given day, there were kids, parents, and/or teachers who were in emergency situations. I became a glorified "fireman." My entire job that year was simply identifying the most pressing fires each day and scurrying around to put them out as effectively as possible.

I'm proud to say that none of the three schools fell apart during that year, but I didn't come close to achieving the level of success that I'd had when I was principal of just Washington, or even when I took over Moody. While they all maintained their state-level designations and didn't slip down to lower levels, there certainly wasn't any significant growth that would move them toward a higher designation. They all survived that school year—that's the best I can say.

FROM ALMOST QUITTING TO FINDING VISION

I contemplated quitting many times during that year of my three-school principalship. I felt like I was horrible at my job because all I was doing was holding things together on a daily basis. I had no time to be proactive about anything, and felt like I was constantly running behind. I felt like a building manager instead of an instructional leader. One of the elements that made my first three years at Washington School so amazing was that we always made time for fun. We tended to the culture of the school to make sure everyone was happy and enjoying the work. During the year split between three schools, culture and fun fell by the wayside. I'd never wanted to be in a career where I just survived, and somewhere around January or February, I seriously contemplated quitting the profession completely.

Thankfully, I didn't quit, because the next school year, two principals were hired—one for each of the smaller buildings. I was to be the principal of the Pawtucketville School. In other words, three principals were now covering what I had been doing alone the previous year.

Up to this point on my leadership journey, I had learned so many essential elements about what it means to be an effective leader. At Washington School I learned the importance of connecting with people and finding my authentic administrative voice. When I was split between the schools I learned the importance of finding ways to delegate and not bear the responsibility of solving all of the problems alone at each school.

Out of the three schools, Pawtucketville was the most challenging. The school had not made significant academic growth in a number of years and was consistently ranked among the bottom 10 percent of schools in the state. Prior to my arrival, they had been identified for Corrective Action or restructuring by the state.

The school culture among the Pawtucketville School faculty was tough. It was known in the city as a difficult place to work. There was a toxic feeling in the building and a high level of teacher turnover. There was a lot of pressure on the teachers by their colleagues to maintain the status quo and not go above and beyond the basic expectations of their jobs. This was frustrating to me. The school had poor student achievement results overall, so I didn't understand why there was such a desire to maintain the status quo. I had been hired the previous year to shake things up. My administrative voice was strong and well developed at that point, plus I had a ton of energy for the work. During year two, after being relieved of my other responsibilities, I was able to give Pawtucketville the kick in the butt it needed.

In order to be effective, teachers need to have the ability to make their own decisions and at this point the school culture was not allowing them to do that on many levels. One tangible example was that teachers were pressured by some colleagues to leave the school almost immediately after the students left.

My goal in the early stages was to do what was right for the students, regardless of the pushback I got from resistant teachers. I wasn't going to battle with those toxic forces over small issues. Instead, I was going to lead the charge and empower the teachers in the building who wanted to move the school forward and who wanted to break up the status quo. Issues like teachers feeling pressured by their colleagues to leave work immediately after the bell seemed to disappear as more and more teachers who had previously been marginalized by the loud, toxic voices, began to feel empowered and protected. Instead of asking directly for a change in behavior, I created an environment that empowered the teachers who wanted to stay.

There were a lot of small victories in that second year at Pawtucketville. I began to learn about the true power of setting both short- and long-term goals. At that point, one of my mentors in the district started pushing me to verbalize my vision more effectively to my faculty. He was adamant that the vision needed to come before anything else in rebuilding or turning around a school, but I actually disagreed. I didn't, and still don't believe that vision can be established by a person who is new to the school. When I took over Pawtucketville it wasn't really a school, it was more like a collection of classrooms that happened to be in the same building. Each classroom was its own island and the only voices being heard were coming from what I call the "status quo guardians." How could one voice bring people together behind any kind of vision in that kind of environment?

We needed to get to know one another and establish a culture of mutual respect. I wanted to create an environment where people were enjoying teaching students. That year, we didn't talk much about instruction, content, or curriculum; the focus was on the mindsets of students and adults. We focused on our own mindsets about success and what we needed to do to help move the school forward: How do we get the kids to want to do better? How do we get our faculty to want to be better? In those discussions, we kept coming back to the fact that neither students nor staff were having fun at school. They didn't enjoy being there, so there was no motivation to work hard.

Starting that year and continuing to this very day, my first and last newsletter to faculty begins with the quote, "If it's not fun, why do it?"—a mantra I borrowed from ice cream legends Ben & Jerry. At Pawtucketville that second year, we spent a lot of time discussing the question; "If you guys aren't enjoying this work and challenging yourself to get better, why are you here?" I had these conversations whenever possible: in grade-level meetings, full-staff meetings, individual evaluation meetings with teachers, and after-classroom observations. I'd make an observation to a teacher about a lesson or other aspect of the school: "You didn't seem to enjoy that very much." The teacher would often respond with, "Well you know, I don't really like doing it that way." So I'd tell them to do it differently. Those discussions led to a seismic shift in the school culture where teachers were now being allowed to make decisions in how they approached their classrooms.

I got pushback from the union and from my central office administration for allowing people to do things differently, but I held tight to the belief that we would get results if we were just allowed to start making our own decisions around the work we do in our building. I stole Spider Man's catchphrase, "With great power comes great responsibility." We were taking chances and rebuilding the school culture, but with that power to make decisions and enact change, came the responsibility of accountability. We needed to own our work and our decisions.

There was internal pushback from the status quo guardians who had previously been the schools most powerful voices. They weren't comfortable with the power being shifted to a different group of teachers, but during the middle of that year, it was clear that the school was at a tipping point. The true vision of the school began to form when I, along with a coalition of teachers, decided that we wanted to move the school forward. It couldn't have been done in the first year or even until the middle of the second year because in my opinion, developing the vision needed to incorporate a core element of the entire faculty. It couldn't just be generated by the principal: the new guy in town

CONFRONTING THE OLD SYSTEM

I could see a lot of great things starting to take shape at Pawtucketville, but there were still many obstacles on our path to success. The status quo guardians were elevating their voices and pushing back in many different ways so I took the biggest leadership risk of my career. I stood up in front of the entire staff and said, "Here's the deal. The school is changing, so you can either choose to stay on board and we'd love to have you, or you can leave right now." I explained that anyone who stayed would be choosing to be a part of the hard work we were doing to move the school forward. I continued, "There are a lot of jobs open in the city right now, so if you want to leave, I'll write you a letter of recommendation."

It was an incredible risk for a relatively young administrator to essentially tell an experienced faculty to get on board or get out of the way. I added an additional element to that decree. I told them, "We need to start doing things differently. If you choose to stay, I'm going to start strategically moving people to different positions in the school where I think they can be more effective. If you want to keep your current job and be a teacher in the classroom you're in at the grade level you're at, you need to learn to enjoy the work. And more importantly, you need to earn your position. Show me that you're passionate about it."

I had thrown down the gauntlet, and for several weeks I wasn't sure which way it would fall. Would my decree work at empowering the positive faculty in the school who wanted change? I knew I had a core group of around eight people solidly in my corner. There was another, much larger group of teachers who were on the fence and could be swayed to either join the new regime or to side with the status quo guardians. I didn't know if I had enough people to tip the scales in my direction, but at that moment for the growth of our school, I knew I needed to try something drastic. It was a massive risk.

Over the next few weeks, many people came into my office freely and gave me feedback—both positive and negative. I listened to everyone and gave them a chance to speak their mind, but I never wavered from the notion that this school was moving forward and that things were going to be done differently.

THE CULTURE OF FUN

We had laid down the foundation for our new vision focused on creating and fostering a culture in the building where both students and staff enjoyed being at our school. After many years of reflecting, it really is that simple: when you create an environment where people feel good, where they want to be part of the success and see the school moving forward, then success will inevitably follow. They find themselves saying, "Hey, I'm enjoying being a part of this, and this is MY work!" The work becomes more doable and people see achieving successes—small and large—as more realistic. Once the success stories start rolling in, striving for growth becomes addictive.

This is not to say that effective leadership simply means making sure that everyone is having fun all the time but in my opinion, being capable of fun is a foundational element. At Pawtucketville, we did a lot of things outside of school to create camaraderie and positive school culture. We had inter-staff basketball or softball games, went to trivia together, or had badminton competitions. We had talent shows and dance competitions or just went out for meals together. At first it was just three, four, five people going to these "shenanigans" as they would later be termed, but by the end of the year there were so many people on our trivia teams that we got kicked out of the bar! The culture was growing fast. Some of my principal colleagues laughed at our frivolity in those first few years, thinking it was a useless waste of our energy, but it absolutely was not useless. These "shenanigans" became an essential part of our school's culture.

That second year at Pawtucketville School, everything came together for me as a leader and my true personal vision was established. That vision would help advance student achievement at Pawtucketville from being in the lowest 10 percent of schools in the state, to being over the 50th percentile just four years later. We were nationally recognized for effective student growth and also by the *Boston Globe* as a "model that works" for turning around a school. During those formative years implementing our school vision, we completely focused ourselves on establishing a culture in the school where people were enjoying their work, where people were allowed to take chances, and where people had fun.

From Philosophy to Practice

We moved out of the danger zone of being a Level 4 school and kicked off year 3 with renewed confidence. The first year I joined Pawtucketville School–the split year–we only moved from around the fourth to the ninth percentile in the state. The second year, we moved up to the 15th percentile. That growth still wasn't great, but it bumped us from a Level 4 to a Level 3. The state would be giving us back complete control of our school.

The third year, we moved beyond establishing our vision and forming our team. We moved beyond getting our mindsets in sync and began fostering a positive culture in our building. We started putting specific structures into place that would support our work, challenge our teachers, and take our instruction to the next level.

Implementing New Structures to Improve Faculty Engagement and Student Learning

That year we tackled a major issue: coaching. Teachers indicated that they wanted instructional coaching and professional development, which they weren't getting from the district at the time. Most importantly, they wanted a voice in how things were going to work around the school.

When we formally implemented a structured coaching model, my resources were decent but not great. I had a literacy specialist and a part-time math resource teacher. My assistant principal and I were the original "model" teachers and participated in every coaching session to help establish the process and open up authentic discussions about what effective instruction looked like in a classroom. At that point, I was six or seven years away from teaching, so I was rusty, and the teachers knew they were better than me in the classroom. The goal was not for my assistant or myself to model good teaching, but instead to establish a process of diagnostic coaching and feedback. They were excited that we were putting ourselves on the line like that and were probably thinking, "Well, obviously I could do better than that!" So the fear of coaching started growing smaller.

I didn't want them to be scared of being vulnerable. They wanted to be better but, as most people are, they were nervous about opening themselves up to potential criticism. My assistant principal and I showed them that it was OK to be anxious and it was OK to receive critical feedback. Making ourselves vulnerable in front of our staff established our coaching model. About halfway through the year, teachers started stepping into the modeling role and being open to feedback. By the beginning of year 4, more than half of the faculty was actively involved in the coaching model and, by the beginning of year 5, we had a formal plan incorporating every teacher in the model.

That instructional tool could never have been built, implemented, and established without first spending a few years building the culture of trust at the school. This coaching was not forced on the faculty and it was not a requirement. Instead, the teachers were pushing for a structure to help them grow as professionals. In the end, everyone wanted to be a part of the model. Whether they were genuinely interested or because they didn't want to feel left out, it didn't matter. Daily coaching sessions became a part of the fabric of our school culture.

Articulating the Vision

That same year, we formally articulated our school's vision statement. We wanted representation from every part of the school, every grade level, and every faculty position. Ultimately, every constituency in the building was represented on the vision drafting team, save one key group—I didn't get parents involved, but that was because I wasn't ready to bring them "behind the curtain" yet.

The leadership team took the work that we did over the past two years and tried to encapsulate it into a formal statement representing our school's vision and purpose. They would then return to their teams for feedback. We would regroup and reword the vision statement based on the feedback, then begin the process again. It took a solid four months of constant revisions, but by Christmas time, we finally had a solid draft. We held an open forum about the vision at the following faculty meeting. The leadership team revised it once more, and developed it into language everybody felt comfortable endorsing, embracing, and implementing within their classroom.

The whole atmosphere in the building had changed. When I walked down the hallways, people were having fun. Kids were smiling, and there were consistently fewer behavioral challenges. Teachers seemed to be enjoying the lessons much more and were actually conversing in the hallways instead of hiding behind closed doors. I brought in a couple of experienced people who I knew would be positive cultural game changers. Teacher turnover decreased, and there were fewer and fewer positions open at the school each year.

Although the status quo guardians would constantly complain, their voices and impact on the school were now marginalized. A principal friend once told me that having fewer cynics is one of a principal's biggest goals. We had successfully shifted the majority mindset in the building. A lot of people who had previously been on the fence had gotten on board. While previously we had spent the whole day talking about the school's problems, we were now able to acknowledge the challenges and collaborate on a game plan to address them.

Formally articulating the vision was really the nail in the coffin for the old practices and mentalities at Pawtucketville. It was built slowly on a foundation of trust and, because everyone had a hand in crafting the vision, it was something they supported and took accountability for. Although we were unaware of it at the time, our student achievement scores that year took off like a rocket ship! In just three short years the school went from the 4th to the 30th percentile. Over the two subsequent years, our school would break into the 50th percentile and continue to grow from there.

LOSING CONTROL—IN A GOOD WAY

The moment I knew the building was heading for great success was the same moment I lost control of the school in the best possible way. The past few years spent building up faculty to combat the status quo guardians had empowered those same teachers to make decisions all over the building. Suddenly, my role became finding ways to implement the teachers' ideas and make them a reality in the classrooms. The faculty was no longer afraid to take chances and go back to the drawing board if an idea failed.

Student achievement at our school truly began to take off toward the end of the year. I realized it wasn't the principal or the administration that effectively moved a school forward, it was empowering faculty to take the responsibility for making effective decisions throughout the building. The principal's role in that work was to help assess what's working and what isn't, and to make the new ideas and approaches a reality in the classrooms.

MISSION ACCOMPLISHED: YEARS 4 AND 5

The next two years at Pawtucketville came and went in a flash. We absolutely hit the ground running in year 4 and the coaching model took off like gangbusters. Teachers were working with our coaches and in each other's classrooms almost daily. They would bring their ideas to us for coaching opportunities. My role became finding the coverage, resources or support they needed to make their ideas work.

While the philosophy of fun and the notion of putting culture first may have been born during my years at Washington School, it came to life and grew into adulthood at Pawtucketville. The majority of the faculty was now unabashedly positive and solution oriented. By the time year 5 rolled around, I honestly felt almost completely useless at the school because the teachers had become so self-sufficient. My main role became defending them from any district initiatives that didn't fit our work at the school and supporting them with student behaviors and challenging parents. They were making the decisions and choosing the school's direction; they were the driving force behind its success. That year we broke into the 50th percentile in the state and were one of the highest-functioning elementary schools in the district.

In particular, our English language learners' growth was astronomical and was one of the primary reasons the school was identified as a Title 1 nationally recognized school. This award is given to schools that have used the Title 1 funds to foster incredible growth in their student populations. In our case, it was a combination of our overall student achievement and growth within our ELL population.

TIME FOR A NEW CHALLENGE

It took me almost a decade to put together all the pieces of what it meant to be an effective leader and to find my own personal voice as an administrator. Those last two years at Pawtucketville were amazing and completely solidified my core values. Solid school culture and community were the foundation of my vision, and everything else grew from that base.

I had spent years pushing my faculty outside their comfort zone and having them take on enormous challenges. I needed to model that mentality in my own career. After five years at Pawtucketville, it was time for a new challenge that would help me grow as a leader and educator.

Wang Middle School, right next door, was the perfect opportunity and middle school leadership would be a brand-new world for me. The Wang School was in a much more stable place than Pawtucketville was when I took over. The previous principal, who had been there fourteen years, had established a solid foundation and put many successful systems into place. Also, Pawtucketville Elementary was a feeder school for the Wang Middle, so I was familiar with many of the parents and kids who attended the Wang.

The retiring principal was a mentor of mine and had done an amazing job with the Wang School. During her last few years, they had plateaued at the Level 2 state designation—just one step away from the top designation. She was extremely invested in getting Wang School to the top of the metaphorical mountain, but the district was getting more and more challenging to navigate, and she was ready for a personal change in her life. Our leadership styles were almost polar opposites, but we both felt that shaking up the school's leadership would be the key to getting Wang to the top of the mountain.

My role as the leader of the Wang School was completely different than it had been at Pawtucketville, where I'd had my hands in everything: instruction, coaching, behavior management, and most other aspects of the school. In the middle school setting, I had to learn how to delegate and depend on the people around me. I had to build trust with them if we were going to move Wang forward. I learned the importance of surrounding yourself with strong team members.

Prior to her departure, the previous principal had hired new curriculum coaches who really helped form the core of my administrative team. The team also stretched to include my assistant principal, school clerk, senior custodian, and guidance counselor. We became interchangeable in our roles at the school. On any given day, this team was dynamically covering whatever needs arose in the building, and slowly that mentality crept into the general faculty population.

FROM GOOD ENOUGH TO GREAT

The Wang School had its own status quo guardians. Although they weren't as toxic as their peers at Pawtucketville, their mentality was actually harder to address because it was coming from very effective teachers. There was a lingering mentality that what they had been doing so far was pretty good, so why change it? The previous principal created an extremely well-functioning school, so instilling a sense of urgency for change was difficult.

My first step was differentiating myself from the prior principal and letting the faculty know that I was going to be doing things differently, not because anything in the past was wrong, but because I was a different kind of leader. In my first big presentation to the faculty—and I actually worked with the prior principal developing this concept—I had a list of about 12 things at the school that we felt needed to change in order to move the school forward. I described how she would have handled or addressed those issues, but then told the faculty, "I'm not going to handle them her way." I was honest in my descriptions of myself as a leader, because I was confident in myself at that point in my career and I had a measure of success that backed up my confidence.

Change progressed slowly at Wang, and it wasn't until year 5 that I actually saw a significant shift in the power structure at the school. Suddenly, a collective and positive voice was driving school decisions rather than the voices of the status quo guardians. After building trust with me as the principal, teachers and staff were feeling comfortable taking risks and were empowered to stand up to the status quo guardians to help move the school forward. At the Wang School, it was never about blowing things up and starting all over. It was about trimming away the parts that weren't working, empowering everyone in the building, and finding a way to continue to help the status quo guardians change their mindset.

Learning from Mistakes

While I'm incredibly proud of the success my schools have had over the years, it is really the mistakes I've made along the way that have helped me truly understand how to be an effective leader. In my first few years at Washington School, I built everything on my own shoulders because I knew the faculty, the parents, and the students depended on me to keep the school moving forward. When suddenly the situation shifted and I had to step away from Washington School, I realized that much of what I had built fell away when I left. Luckily, that small school community was amazing enough to keep the work moving forward without me. My mistake at the Washington School was thinking I had to do everything and be everything that everyone needed.

In hindsight, I am glad I didn't give up and quit after my "split between schools" years. Everything I learned in those first five years in Lowell and every one of my mistakes helped me to become the leader I am today. I knew the school was in a bad place when I was assigned to Pawtucketville, so my mentality out of the gates was, "This is how I do things. Get on board or get the hell out of my way!" Had I replaced the words "I" and "my" with "we" and "our," I may have been able to get more people on board rather than having to chase them out of the building.

After ten years of being an elementary school principal in Lowell, I truly felt completely confident in my ability to be a school leader at Wang Middle School. I knew that I couldn't shoulder the burden of moving the school forward alone, I had to trust people to be a part of the process rather than viewing them just as obstacles. I needed to build an amazing team because this work simply can't be done alone.

I know I've made a lot of individual mistakes with parents, saying things I shouldn't have said because I've got no filter between my brain and my mouth. I wish in some cases I had handled my faculty issues with a more human approach. There were times where I was so focused on moving the school forward that I lost track of the individuals who make up our school community. My social worker from my first few years at Washington School once said to me, "You have a very effective administrative toolbox. The issue is, all you have is hammers—you have different size hammers for different things around the school, but they're all hammers." That advice has stuck with me, because while I have not been extremely successful at diversifying my administrative toolbox beyond just "hammers," I now surround myself with people who have completely different leadership toolboxes. A school needs all different approaches, not just hammers.

The most important lesson that I carry with me today is that effective leadership is NOT perfect. You make mistakes as a leader, and how you handle those mistakes demonstrates more about you as a leader than anything else. Do you blame others for the mistakes? Do you run from accountability? Or do you reflect on what you could have done better and make a change? The best thing I did to build my confidence and to be an effective leader for my schools was to never give up. It's really that simple—never give up. The work in schools is not easy and it can often be even more challenging in urban settings, so leaders must not only foster the mentality of perseverance, they must model it for their students and faculty. It's OK to make mistakes, it's part of the process. However, it's never OK to give up. That is what I take with me from my administrative journey and what I try to model now for my faculty. I am not a perfect leader and I don't strive to be, but no matter what the challenge, I will be standing with them shoulder-to-shoulder trying to keep the school moving forward.

REFLECTIONS ON LEADERSHIP

In my experience, principals can expect to interact with three categories of people in the school community. From a leader's perspective, the first group is the most comfortable; the hope is that this group eventually becomes the biggest group in the building. These are the people who you know are standing shoulder-to-shoulder with you in whatever you face at your school, because they like you as a person and they respect the work you are doing.

The second group is a little more uncomfortable for leaders. People in this group might not like you personally, but they have tremendous respect for the work that is being done around the building and want to be a part of moving it forward. As a human being, it is difficult for leaders to know that they are potentially not liked as a result of the decisions they need to make. However, even if they don't like the leader as a person, this second group will still follow a leader and stand shoulder-to-shoulder with them if they have respect for the work that is being done.

The last group is by far the most uncomfortable for a leader. The hope is that this group grows smaller and smaller with each passing year. Like the second group, they may not like the leader as a person, but more impactfully, they don't have respect for the work that is being done. The status quo guardians tend to fall into this category. Fear is the absolute worst way to manage people, but in my experience, the only way to keep this group from tearing apart a school's culture is if they are afraid of the consequences of doing so. Ideally, a leader earns the respect of this group and they move into the second group, where they become a part of the school's success instead of an obstacle.

After well over a decade of leadership, I am not only comfortable in my skills as a leader but strong in my belief that school culture must come first to build the foundation for success. While my "shenanigans" were not taken seriously by other leaders early in my career, they have become a districtwide initiative so many years later because they have had such a positive impact on the schools where I've been a principal.

As I reflect on my leadership journey, I've learned that it is absolutely essential to have a strong vision, a clear voice, and confidence in your ability to lead. This doesn't mean being perfect or shouldering all the burden, but it means standing up for what is right and doing whatever is needed to move a school forward. In that work, you must accept that you are not always going to be the most popular person in the building.

My leadership journey really is summed up by the combination quotes from Douglas Adams and Ben & Jerry. I never thought I would end up as an educator and I never believed myself to be a leader, but with the lessons I've learned along the way, I can agree with Douglas Adams: "I may not have gone where I intended to go, but I think I have ended up where I needed to be." On the other hand, if this work wasn't fun and I didn't enjoy it, I'm not sure I would have survived those years when I was split between schools, so Ben & Jerry had it right when they said, "If it's not fun, why do it?"

After a year of juggling the leadership of three schools simultaneously, Matt was able to focus all his attention on Pawtucketville School. Matt noted that the culture in the building was "toxic"; dominated by "status quo guardians" whose strong voices discouraged change. Teachers worked in isolation; each classroom was an island. After learning from teachers that they weren't having fun teaching and didn't enjoy being in the building, Matt actively worked to "empower and protect" teachers who wanted to move the school forward. He posited that when people enjoyed what they were doing, their motivation to collaborate around school improvement would increase. Matt focused his discussions with faculty on countering their feedback that neither teachers nor students were having fun at school. His goal was to encourage teachers to incorporate having fun into their instruction.

But Matt asked himself: Did the faculty know how to have fun? Assuming some deficiency Matt offered the faculty myriad afterschool recreational activities, ranging from trivia contests to badminton for their voluntary participation. The initial skepticism as to the value of fun times morphed into a school wide engagement in fun activities. The application of having fun to engaging in fulfilling work was a high prospect.

Matt coalesced the Pawtucketville faculty around his vision that teaching infused with fun would improve student learning. He established strong interpersonal relationships with the faculty. He promoted ongoing adult learning in the school. He posed the question, "If you aren't enjoying this work and challenging yourself, why are you here?" communicating his perspective around the opportunities for change and responsibility for students's success that is at the heart of teaching.

Those who signed on to Matt's vision shifted their thinking about how to teach. He understood that highly motivating classrooms should balance the methods teachers use with the content students were expected to learn. He reasoned that if teachers enjoyed their work and found creative and "fun" approaches to instruct their students, then the students would engage with the material in exciting ways and their learning would increase. His approach invited faculty members to take appropriate risks and try strategies they thought would infuse fun into their classrooms while moving student learning forward. Matt countered pushback from the central office leadership and the teachers' association. He advocated for teacher autonomy and ownership of decision-making at the school level.

Matt's message communicated to the "status quo guardians" of the faculty that his style was different from previous leaders. He offered an audacious choice to all faculty. One could remain in the building and continue to integrate fun into their teaching or one could request a transfer to another school in the district with Matt's recommendation assured. He was transparent in stating that by choosing to remain in the school faculty would have to embrace his vision of weaving fun into their instruction so that both adults and students experience it. The majority of teachers chose to remain in the building, a vote of confidence in Matt's vision of enhanced student learning.

When the teachers requested curriculum coaching to expand their skills Matt volunteered to be coached, modeling vulnerability by teaching in front of his faculty. His actions increased the self-confidence of the faculty who joined the process. Teachers delivered inspired instruction that increased student engagement in learning, built excitement around new approaches to learning and improved student achievement. The school moved from a low level of academic achievement to the top tier as measured by the annual state assessments.

3

Henry Turner

Bedford High School

2012-2016

Newton North High School

2016-present

Leadership Story

I've always had an interest in leadership, starting in high school and then in college. I became a teacher to help make a difference for kids who don't have all the necessary resources to be successful.

Fresh out of college, I started teaching at Mohawk Trail Regional High School in Western Massachusetts before transitioning to Lexington High School, where I spent seven years. The achievement gap in Lexington was glaringly evident; I was interested in changing that. I worked with a range of students—those who were MIT and Harvard-bound and others who were struggling to finish high school. The gap was astounding, and I quickly made a reflection that continues to shape my work to this day. The student of a doctor knows the process of becoming a doctor. Parents without a high school degree have a much harder time illuminating paths for their student. Schools can be a huge support.

My time spent at Lexington High was an awakening. I realized that I could have a career in leadership. I wanted to be a change agent and applied to the Educator Leadership Institute (ELI). The ELI experience helped me become a better teacher and leader. What I learned there was invaluable. I learned how to think about and effectively use data; how to identify achievement gaps in order to understand where students were struggling, and how to create change both inside and outside the classroom. I became obsessed with the intellectual aspects of leadership.

GETTING IN THE DOOR

I applied for several administrative positions but was turned down. I wondered if I would spend my whole career at Lexington High. I had to rethink my story as an interviewee—for myself and for the kind of job I wanted. I knew I wanted to lead, but I love teaching and wasn't positive that I wanted to leave the classroom. I applied and was hired for the role of housemaster position at Newton South High School. In that role, I could be a leader while still having the opportunity to teach kids. It was the perfect situation for me.

During my time at Newton South, I worked with a diverse group of students and educators. I gained perspective on the behavioral side of things, which helped me think about the larger scope of leading a school. It was good preparation for becoming a principal.

STARTING AT BEDFORD

After four years at Newton South, I applied for the principalship of Bedford High School. I would have been happy to stay at South, but I felt ready to take on the job in Bedford. I knew there was going to be a lot for me to learn, but I hadn't expected the learning experience to start during the interview process. I wasn't selected during the first round of interviews and had to interview three more times before making it to an on-site meeting with teachers. The process took a couple of months, and as a competitive and confident person, I was taken aback. Not getting that first call shook me up a little. I had to develop a thick skin.

I fell in love with the school after the on-site visit. Bedford had real energy. Although it was a small school, there were plenty of opportunities for everyone there. One thing that attracted me to Bedford was that it was a METCO district [Metropolitan Council for Educational Opportunity, a voluntary school desegregation program]. I grew up in a METCO district and, aside from the year I spent teaching in Western Massachusetts after college, had worked exclusively in METCO districts.

About 13% of Bedford's students at the time lived on or near Hanscom Air Force base, as a number of them came from military families. The student body was economically, racially and culturally diverse, representative of groups from all over the country.

My predecessor was being promoted to Superintendent of Bedford Schools. He had been the high school principal for 12 years, and I knew it would be great to have him as a mentor. We clicked really well from the start; both he and I were all about fostering relationships. During my first week as principal, he invited me for a walk near a pond where he lived and we just shot the breeze. There were several times over the course of that summer where he invited me out for a beer and a talk, and we were able to get to know each other better. It was part of the foundation that allowed us to have a trusting relationship. Every principal will have moments when they want to go into their predecessor's office and ask, "What were you thinking when you did this?" If the trust level is there, you can. He was able to give me clarification or the backstory on some of the people I was tangling with. Before I delivered my entry plan to the faculty, I was able to run it by him so he could identify potential controversies.

ENTRY PLAN

The very first thing I did after being hired was develop an entry plan. Joel Stembridge, who was my mentor and principal at Newton South, offered excellent advice: identify the seasoned veterans and build relationships with them because generally they're the ones who run the school. I reached out to those folks at the beginning of my entry process, sending several of them my entry plan for feedback.

One of the first people I emailed was the longtime guidance director, who was a very powerful player in the school. I sent her a copy of my entry plan and asked for any feedback or suggestions. She was pleasantly surprised that I had sought her advice. It was a great first step toward building our relationship.

I attempted similar outreach with the rest of the leadership team, who represented a mix of sixteen administrators and teachers. As a group, they had appeared unwieldy during my initial on-site visit, peppering me with disorganized questions. I had a hunch that they were in need of some team building. These were the leaders of the school; we were going to have to give each other straight feedback and be open with each other. I decided to meet with them individually on my entry plan, about 45 minutes each, and get their input. This was a big part of earning my trust with them.

I sent my revised entry plan to the entire staff and asked them to consider some questions: What's going well, and what isn't? What were things they would like to see improve? What would I need to accomplish by next year to be considered successful?

My goal was to have half-hour meetings with all 100 teachers. It would be up to them to decide whether they wanted to meet individually or in small groups. I spent most of June doing rapid-fire interviews with folks, which allowed me to get most of the interviews done. By the first day of school in September, I had met with almost every teacher. It was exhausting, but also an incredible experience. I was doing a lot of listening. I never got to the original questions. We talked about our kids, significant others, where we lived, where we went to school—everything but the actual high school. We shared a lot of personal information; so by the first day of school, I knew a little bit about each faculty member. I could see them at the superintendent's breakfast, address them by name and ask; "How's your sick student doing?"

There was a lot of faculty turnover districtwide, which was affecting the school's climate. Teachers shared with me that change in the school and district was creating anxiety. They wondered what the future would hold for them. My one-on-one conversations with faculty instantly helped build bridges and created a sense of connection during the turnover turmoil.

Over the summer, I surveyed parents, asking them similar questions to those I had asked teachers. In December of that first year, I analyzed the data and presented it to the faculty. There were significant themes of concern that demanded attention

SIGNIFICANT CHALLENGES—THE IPAD PROGRAM

When I took over Bedford, I found two big issues right away. The first was that it was the first year of the new Massachusetts teacher evaluation program, which demanded time-consuming faculty professional development. But a more immediate and complicated challenge was that the district had distributed iPads to all the freshmen without any preparation given to teachers or students on how to use them for student learning. These initiatives came top down and generated real resentment and a sense of powerlessness among faculty. Fostering trust was going to be a huge issue.

The iPad program was headed for disaster and generated a lot of anger. The faculty felt it had been imposed on them, while parents didn't see any rationale for why they were helpful for learning. Parents were also concerned that they would be held responsible if the devices were broken. Although only the freshmen class received iPads, it was an expensive initiative. To make matters worse, the teachers had just agreed to increase their pay contract for the year. I felt pretty isolated because both the tech director and the previous superintendent had left the district. They had been the biggest proponents of the program. Although no one said it, I felt like I had to be the one to make sure it was successful.

GETTING THE ADMINISTRATIVE TEAM ON BOARD

My strategy was to empower the administrative team who would in turn, empower teachers to own how to improve student learning using the technology. I wanted to make it less top-down and have the teachers feel the iPads were an authentic educational tool. Everyone would have their voice in the successful evolution of the program.

I set up half-hour, biweekly meetings with each administrative team member for an informal check-in. There were 16 of them, so it took up a lot of time. A 16-person team was not conducive to collaboration, so I decided to limit the team to just administrators, rather than including teacher leaders. Getting the team down to 10 people was essential in building trust: they could talk about confidential matters without it leaking out. My message to them had always been that loyalty was essential; we could disagree in the room but would always be unified outside it.

My administrative team had really started to pick up steam by the spring of my first year. Some of the key leaders started to say, "I think this guy Henry is really invested."

The department heads were called program administrators (PAs). PAs were basically full-time teachers who did a little bit of administrating. When I arrived at Bedford, they taught three classes instead of the usual five. In my first year, we were able to get them down to teaching one class each. The PAs were still very much viewed as teachers who also did the teaching schedule. Teachers trusted them because they felt the PAs kept the "real" administrators—the principal, superintendent, and the district personnel—at a distance. Some of the PAs were less effective administrators but had the political capital and trust to win the day with their teachers.

I would frequently check in with them rather than waiting for them to come to me with issues. Sometimes during that first year, a problem-solving meeting that was supposed to be 15 minutes ended up being closer to an hour. It would be great in the long run, but it took up a lot of my time and focus. I was slowly building relationships with the program administrators, and I began to understand some of their divisions and their areas of real strength.

Going into my second year, I was able to have more PAs come on board. They had made some progress, but still weren't a healthy body. They were talking to each other more, and some who had previously been silent in meetings started speaking up. I told them that they would need to meet as a team each week, but also "Sometimes I'll be there and sometimes it's going to be just you guys." Before I got to Bedford, their meetings were focused almost exclusively on administrative matters and although they hated it, it was what they were comfortable with. I said, "We're doing the business stuff online. I'm going to approve pretty much every field trip you want. You make the decision, and I'm going to say 'yes.'" Now the business stuff was electronic.

It took them a while to get used to taking ownership of the meetings. When they were meeting without me, they would ask me beforehand, "What's our topic going to be?" I would say, "You are a professional learning community." Then they would ask, "What's our goal going to be?" That year, their goal was their departmental review process. By the end of the year, they were able to change the process substantially. They had tackled a time-consuming, long-term process and did a really nice job. They came to me and asked if they could replace some of our faculty meeting time with peer observations. I said, "Of course, absolutely." Those were some of the signs that the group was starting to click. We were starting to make progress.

There were still some folks in the group who were struggling. It was a mixture of group challenges and sometimes their leadership skills. I think some people felt that it was the time in their career to try something different. Some strong people ended up leaving. Going into my fourth year, there were only three people on the administrative team who I hadn't hired. The group was stronger that year than it had been previously, and I was getting the feeling that people wanted to work with me—they trusted me. Now the PAs were holding each other accountable. They disagreed on a lot of things but were on the same page about our priorities.

I celebrated individual successes when warranted. Behind-the-scenes politics still existed. Some PAs thought they had formed strong relationships with me. I was trying to empower them to help me with the group; but at the same time, they were using that power to jockey for position; to look after themselves. When it came to celebrating the PA group as a whole, I acknowledged how far they had come. From my perspective, they weren't totally united as a team, but they felt accomplished for having gotten something done.

TURNING PROGRAM ADMINISTRATORS INTO PLC LEADERS

The PA team started to unify over developing a plan to handle the iPad issue. We started with a conversation around collaboration: "How do we get teachers to collaborate?" We talked about a Professional Learning Community (PLC) model, and the PAs really started loving the idea of structured discussions around teaching and learning, the essence of a PLC process. I gave them two and a half hours, two Wednesdays a month, contingent on them allowing more time for teachers in their department meetings to talk about teaching and learning through a PLC lens. The bargain worked. It wasn't my initiative, but rather something they felt they needed. Before rolling PLCs out to the teachers, I planned with the PAs behind the scenes. We practiced different types of collaboration. My strategy to get all this accomplished was to empower PAs to collaborate using PLCs as a model. This would provide the long-term path for incorporating iPads into our curricula. Again, I didn't want to make it feel like a top-down initiative. My goal with the iPads was to make them just another learning tool we used.

By getting the PAs to buy into PLCs and make it their initiative, I helped to create strong change agents. I made sure I said, "This was a PA initiative." Some of the PAs couldn't quite believe it would work, but it was something they as a group were all behind and were driving. Part of the buy-in came from offering flexibility for how to use the technology. I wasn't saying, "This is how it's going to be." They had the flexibility to make decisions based on what they thought was best for their departments. Teachers bought into it too.

BUILDING TEACHER TRUST AND COLLABORATION

During my first year, I paid a lot of attention to the administrators on my leadership team. I thought it was going well, but in hindsight I can see that it also kept me from interacting with teachers. I spent a lot of time interacting with PAs behind closed doors. My predecessor had been there a long time, and I don't think he did that. For teachers who were used to being able to drop in, talk, and get support from the PAs, the closed doors must have been scary: "What's he up to?" "What's he going to change?" Building trust with teachers is an ongoing process.

Like the PAs, teachers had no experience with collaboration. My predecessor would use faculty meetings to share very specific topics and teaching strategies that he wanted all teachers to learn. It was all done to teachers. I saw a possible opening for PLCs: the iPads needed to be used as educational tools—and more structured collaboration would help teachers grow.

When I presented to the faculty I explained that iPads were going to be used to focus on student collaboration, critical thinking, and comprehension. This caught the PAs' attention. iPads could be helpful: it was no longer about the technology; it was back to teaching and learning. The budget for my second year included a rollout that would give iPads to more than half our students. Two of the more vocal and more veteran PAs had really bought into the program. They were great supporters of both my vision and where the school was headed. They were from two high-powered departments—science and social studies. I also got support from the English department head who was a powerhouse, quieter but well-respected. For the new folks, their buy-in gave the sense that the team was moving in the right direction.

Between that presentation and the faculty meeting in the spring, teachers had a lot of time to learn from some of our high-flying tech people. They were able to really see what small group structured collaboration could look like. Recognizing that PAs could be a strategic force for change helped us to better engage teachers.

At first, there were only pockets in which collaboration with teachers worked well. I would walk around during classroom time and see some groups of teachers working really well together, while other teachers would be by themselves. I hated having to throw the hammer down on someone for not collaborating—it broke the trust.

Growing Teacher PLCs

Teachers had found their voice, and everyone was really driving the learning. There was now a real energy around PLCs. Most teachers worked in at least one PLC. They had figured out how PLCs could work for them and help in their practice. I was fielding lots of requests for various PLC groups. For example, many freshman teachers had been frustrated with their students, so we had a group focused on sharing best practices for handling challenging students.

Teachers started using teacher time to meet in PLCs. I couldn't touch that time. They were connecting over common interests and working collaboratively. What was happening was fulfilling my vision. There was room for improvement, but things were much better. I no longer needed to use that hammer.

Ed Camp

Ed Camp is the ultimate teacher-centered form of professional learning. In the Ed Camp model, teachers were responsible for selecting and presenting on topics they found relevant. It's a professional development day for teachers where they choose where they go and what to learn. I worried that teachers wouldn't buy into Ed Camp if it was presented by me, so I asked one of our science teachers, who was a technology high-flier, to recruit a committee of teachers to do a creative Ed Camp session. "There's one rule" I said, "It has to be completely teacher-driven. I'm here to help, but don't want to direct anything." She learned to use my help, while doing the lion's share of the work. That community of teachers created a really exciting day for the faculty.

After the second year of Ed Camp, teachers remarked that it was the best professional development they had ever had. Cultural proficiency was a key theme. Last year's most successful professional development initiative revolved around discussions about our students. It had nothing to do with technology. We focused on four areas: race, gender identity, English language learners, and anxiety. Two teachers presented each topic to the rest of the faculty, relaying the students' voices on the topic. Teachers were to talk to students directly and report back: "Here are some things that you can do tomorrow to address the student's concerns." "Here are some things that you should think about long-term." The stakes were pretty high.

After each session, teachers had four options. If the topic was heavy for them, they could go for a walk and gather their thoughts. Alternatively, they could choose to talk to a friend informally. One of the facilitators would hold a session to provide more information for those who still felt unfamiliar with the topic, while the other would hold a high-level session for those who felt like experts. This, in my opinion, was the best part of the entire initiative. Teachers were able to choose what they felt they needed. We were able to incorporate that type of professional learning into all of our PD days. I think teachers really respected that we trusted them to process the information on their own terms.

INSTRUCTIONAL ROUNDS

I introduced Elizabeth City's book *Instructional Rounds*. Two new program administrators, two of the veteran powerhouse PAs, and three relatively new PAs started working together to incorporate instructional rounds in their departments. It was completely driven by them. It was a big step. My first year, they were protecting their fiefdoms, and refused to talk to each other. Our core administrative group was clashing. There was still some history of skepticism and a lack of trust. By the end of my third year, however, they were 100% focused on breaking down the departments' barriers and going into each other's classrooms. It was a real grassroots sort of thing, and some of the teachers started joining them.

SETBACK—BREAKING TRUST

As a school leader, part of my job was building trust: between administrators, teachers, parents, students, and myself. At the end of my third year, I had a setback in my rapport with teachers that was prompted by the administration of the annual district-sponsored feedback survey.

The Bedford Education Association (the teachers union) got involved with this survey because my administrative team, the PAs, and I had become quite close at this point. We had agreed that this was going to be a survey just about our administrative group. The Association was concerned, however, that teachers in the Association were going to see the results.

Although none of the PAs had spoken up at our meetings about the survey, I found out later that at least one of them had voiced a concern with the Association. We were starting to get suspicious of each other. Up until then, our norm was vocalizing concerns and putting them on the table. So I sent out the survey.

Then the Association president followed with an unexpected email to the entire district, saying, "Do not fill out the survey." This created real tension between the Association and me. I worked with the superintendent to figure out how to move past this, and we did, but from my perspective, this one episode challenged our trust with one another.

Eventually, teachers were offered the option of completing the survey. The feedback for the high school was divided between whether or not there was trust between administrators and teachers. I think the ones who took the survey were mostly a small group of disgruntled people. Some of their feedback was pretty brutal. In the end though, a lot of people who had chosen not to take the survey were saying they wished they had, because they didn't feel that way.

This got me thinking about sharing data. Knowing that the PAs were there with me, step-by-step was very encouraging. A lot of them did their own internal surveys in their departments. They had their own struggles with their departments, so it was helpful for them to think about how to respond to negative feedback. They thought I had made a good move. I didn't just sit in my office by myself; I discussed the issue with my PAs when they came in over the summer.

BUILDING TRUST AGAIN—THE TED TALK

One of my summer reads was *TED Talks: How to Talk Like TED.* When the survey issue came up, I started to think: What if I did a TED talk as a way to respond to the trust issue? So my fourth year's opening-day speech was about trust. I practiced my talk with the administrative team. They were so excited and provided good feedback for me.

First, I talked about my viewpoint on change. I asked the faculty to think of the school as a ship. If we turned too hard, we would capsize. If we steered just 10 degrees at a time, we might not see the impact immediately, but it would be evident once we were further out. Some people had fears around the technology, the iPad implementation. I asked them to start making small 10-degree shifts in their practice. If we all made these small shifts, it would have a substantive impact on our practice.

Then I transitioned and began addressing this idea of trust. I pulled up the year 3 survey results, where there had been this tension around if there was mutual respect among administrators and teachers. I emphasized that trust is a two-way street and acknowledged that myself, along with the program administrators, needed to do something differently. I said to them, "If I've done anything to hurt your trust and respect, I'm sorry. I want to know what I did so I can fix it." I apologized to those who felt like I hadn't communicated with them enough. I told them that they needed to do something as well: "If you feel like I'm unapproachable, I'm sorry, try me again." I was vulnerable with them. After the presentation, people came to me saying, "You hit everything perfectly. It was really right on!" When you have low points, it's the team that can pick you up.

I felt very pleased I wasn't driving the boat anymore and, in some ways, I was becoming dispensable. It was a good thing, because it meant I was helping them. For example, the group that wanted to present to the team on instructional rounds had a presentation that really didn't look very good, so they presented to me first and they asked for my thoughts. My new role was coaching, not dictating.

My relationship with the Association had improved too. I wasn't sure that was going to happen. We had a good relationship up until the survey crisis. Looking back, I can see that it had just been a bump in the road.

THE ACHIEVEMENT GAP

Thinking about student achievement brings me back to the data team presentation and our school improvement plan. The first year, my vision was how iPads were going to be used to focus on key areas of student collaboration like critical thinking and comprehension. My focus the second year was on using the iPads and continuing our common assessment work. Going into my third year, I identified that there were gaps between our highest-level and middle-level classes related to race, economic class, and where kids lived. Kids from Boston, in the METCO program, were underrepresented in our high honors and AP classes. In response to this, the faculty voted to select one thing we could do as a school and one thing teachers could do in their classrooms to respond to the gaps.

We came up with two action items: to improve communication and to hold high expectations for all students. The communication component was to foster more communication between teachers within the school but also with parents. With respect to expectations, we realized we had to address our program-of-studies rubric, which was very antiquated. We discussed ways in which high honors AP created hurdles for students.

We were able to embed "checking for understanding" into our rubric for the teacher evaluation. We used the iPads a lot during those first two years to help assess levels of student understanding. I gave teachers about four weeks to try using an app that focused on checking for student's understanding. We introduced the app to the kids, and the next day, one of them said, "I just used Socrato [learning analytics and standardized test scoring software] in every single one of my classes."

We had finally gotten the focus back to student achievement. By year 3, technology was just how we did business. We didn't have a technology coach, but rather an instructional coach. The third- and fourth-year school improvement plans were more academically focused, and we could emphasize communication and high achievement for students rather than technology. It was all centered around our achievement gap.

One of our measures was on the state achievement tests:MCAS. When I entered, 100% of our students were proficient or advanced in English language arts, so we were already doing well. But we started using MCAS as a measure to determine if students of color were improving. We also measured the number of students of color moving into some of our upper-level classes and really building momentum in that area. We began offering more opportunities and electives to students. We created a number of programs, particularly within our special education department, that supported students around mental health. We saw an increase in social-emotional well-being.

REFLECTIONS ON BEDFORD

When you're leaving a school, there's a selfish opportunity to really hear people's thoughts about you. I identified a dozen very experienced teachers to give me honest feedback face-to-face. I asked them to tell me about when I was at my best and when Iwas at my worst. I chose people I knew would be honest. People liked that I was "a listener," and I felt proud of that. They felt that when I listened to them, I was really absorbing what they had to say.

One accomplishment was that I got a solid leadership team working collaboratively and really functioning. We were successful in enacting some positive changes for kids at the school. We built momentum over the course of the years, from creating courses that were unleveled for students which was a big change, to providing more flexibility and types of assessments that teachers were giving for midyear exams. I think those changes stemmed from having a functioning team.

I'm really proud of student outcomes during my time in Bedford. We were recognized by the state for closing achievement gaps. I didn't claim it as my success—it was the school's success. Through the PLC work, sharing strategies, the infusion of technology, and allowing students to try different learning methods, teachers had a lot of opportunities.

In terms of mistakes, I think that I focused a lot on the administrative team because the former team hadn't worked well. Although getting a strong, functioning admin team was one of the things I'm proudest of, focusing so much on them challenged my relationships with some of the faculty. I think it was a culture shift for the faculty to see an empowered administrative team. Some people struggled with the change, in part because I didn't take my time and go a little slower. I wanted to get into some new initiatives; to try something unknown. They just felt like we didn't have all the answers. I was pushing ahead and they were responding, "We're going too fast."

There are things that are going to go wrong as a leader, right? You really don't establish yourself as a principal until you've gone through some challenging situations. When some of those challenging situations occur, your relationships evolve. Building those individual relationships with peers, and faculty was crucial in building trust

Decision to Leave Bedford

After three years in Bedford, I applied for and was offered the principalship at Newton North High School. Newton felt like my administrative home as years previously, my first position as an administrator had been at Newton South, the other high school in the district. I knew both the community and the politics. It seemed like a good fit and an intriguing challenge.

I was looking forward to the challenges that accompanied a larger and more diverse school. Newton North's principal at the time had a big personality. From my experiences at Newton South and at Bedford,

I had practice with having to replace big personalities. It was a good kind of challenge.

I think that Newton and I are a good match in terms of my vision for a school overall, its culture, and its commitment to students. My experience with technology and emphasis on student learning matches well with Newton North. I'm also a believer in fate, and the position had been open for a year, so it just felt like it was the right decision.

My last year at Bedford, when I knew I was leaving, I did a lot of exit surveys around the trust issue. By the end, I felt very strongly that the overwhelming majority of teachers had a trusting relationship with me. It was hard ending all the relationships that I had built. A lot of the young administrators I had hired really took the job, trusting that I was going to be there for a while and that I would mentor them. Exiting Bedford was harder than entering North. As a leader, it was really challenging to lose that political capital toward the end. Figuring out the transition was a huge new challenge, and it took a lot of my effort.

Entry into Newton North

I created an entry plan similar to the one I had used in Bedford. I was committed to the idea that personal relationships would really help me. The question was how to go about developing those relationships at a larger school. Like Bedford, I put together a survey. There was a lot of participation: I had 550 respondents. It was pretty open-ended. Questions like, "What does 'Tiger Pride' mean to you?" "What's working well?" "What are some things that need to be addressed?" "What would a successful first year for me look like?"

I created opportunities throughout the spring, summer, and fall for people to meet with me individually. While there wasn't 100% participation, many people responded. Getting to know them was a huge help.

My opening speech to the faculty that year was another TED talk, but it differed from the one I had given in Bedford. For a lot of Bedford teachers, I had moved too fast. At times, people felt there was a lack of focus. Newton North, however, was doing well. The faculty worked well together. There was less pressure for me to provide a strategic plan immediately. That first year, I was clear and deliberate with the faculty about what I was doing: "This is a complex school—I'm taking this year to get to know it."

I created a "Wordle" of answers to "What does 'Tiger Pride' mean to you?" Words like community, support, accomplishments, education, spirit, students, teachers, pride, and respect were all strung together in this word collage that I felt really captured the culture of the school. It created an image that we could all unite around. I think it set the tone for my priorities and leadership style. My goals were to really learn about the school. I understood that Newton North had great pride in its history and traditions. I wanted to learn how to become part of the community.

I explained that I wanted this to be collaborative and that innovation would be encouraged. Although I didn't have a finalized strategic plan, I already knew some of my key themes: collaboration, relationships, and innovation.

The Entry Crisis

It was an unexpectedly challenging entry. I was learning about the school and planning to take my time doing so, but racist and political incidents forced me into decision mode. The week school started, some students took the opportunity to drive around campus waving Confederate flags. I told the faculty, "This is our issue." We needed to make cultural proficiency and anti-bias work a priority. I mentioned a few high-profile incidents that had occurred the previous year, before I had taken over as principal. There was anti-Semitism, with a big incident at a basketball game where some kids from another school jeered at our kids, "You killed Jesus." And there were some racist incidents at one of our assemblies.

I leveled with the faculty; having conversations about race is really difficult. I shared a story about an interaction I had with my daughter. One afternoon on our way home from kindergarten, she said she didn't have school on Monday because it was Martin Luther King's birthday. I asked her if she knew who Martin Luther King was, and she said, "In the olden days, people with black skin and people with white skin couldn't drink out of the same water fountains, and he fixed that." I followed up, "Do you know anyone in our family who has black skin?" She said, "Who?" I told her, "Papa and daddy and you." Then she asked, "What about mommy?" I said, "No, not mommy," and she said, "I want to be like mommy." I said, "In the olden days, people like mommy and daddy would not have been able to get married and that Martin Luther King helped fix that too." She said, "What would have happened?" I paused and I said, "We might have gone to jail." She went, "Dada, don't talk about this anymore. You can tell me when I'm older." It was a lot for her, and hard to hear. That interaction had been in January, and in June, she came home with a painting. It read "I see my blue eyes and rosy cheeks. My face is unique and special." So she had been thinking about it this whole time.

I continued my entry talk: "Regardless of their race, every kid walks through these halls with a unique story. In order to be comfortable with that and talk about that, we need to take risks." The message was that teachers should be having conversations with kids to support them in embracing their unique identities. It went really well.

I keep my daughter's painting in my office so that people remember that story. As a first-year principal, I hadn't thought about that kind of learning for adults. Now I was constantly thinking about how to continue this message. People forget when things are going well. I am constantly embedding different ways to help them remember the message.

One of the challenges of my first year was that we were instantly thrown into crisis mode. In some ways, it was good because we bonded as a team. But at the same time, it sort of took us off course in terms of doing the reflection and learning I had wanted to do during my entry.

ANTI-BIAS PROGRAMS

After the first week of school, the big questions were, "How do we take this on as a community?" and "How do we build a school that makes sure that all students develop social and civic learning skills?" I started working with the students immediately. After the flag incident, some students were threatening to walk out of school in protest, which I thought was unsafe. At 9:00 on a Thursday night, I negotiated the terms with a group of 16-year-olds. By Friday morning, we were closer to a compromise. We needed to find a place for them to have their voices heard. We had them hold a rally in the cafeteria, rather than stage a walkout. It was more consistent with what we could support. We made sure it was a big event. I was there, faculty were there. They had some speakers, and it was packed. It sent a message that the school's leadership supported students' voices. The rally created activism among our students. At the same time, we were figuring out how to support students without disrupting the school.

We held meetings with a smaller group of kids and were making some headway. But the tension kept mounting throughout the year. A Boston-area TV show highlighted some of our Donald Trump–supporting students. We had some offensive graffiti, and some nasty comments were made between students during some of our assemblies.

So over the course of my first year, social and civic learning remained our priority. Some things we did were symbolic. For example, a group of students designed a mural reflective of our mission statement. But we also made some substantive changes. We changed our anti-bullying curriculum to an anti-bias curriculum and challenged teachers to identify social and civic skills they felt students should learn in their classes. Teachers were tasked with helping students develop in those areas.

I created a committee of passionate teachers and students who were committed to getting an anti-bias curriculum integrated into our school. Twice a year, we would stop the typical schedule, and students would spend time in their homeroom working on the curriculum. The committee created it, and students facilitated; for instance, some of our juniors would spend time working with the freshman. It was really exciting.

I think my response to those incidents established my legitimacy among the faculty. Even though I hadn't set my strategic vision yet, the faculty realized that I knew what I was doing.

Questions around the incidents and the issue of bias started me on the path to a plan. I'd been thinking about the skills the kids needed to have in this environment. One night, it occurred to me that I had never seen the school's mission statement. After reading it, I realized that it laid out some really nice expectations around social and civic expectations. I started creating a strategic plan.

Our goal that year as an administrative team was to provide some professional development on anti-bias for our teachers. We rolled out a plan for how to double down on our social and civic expectations for kids. We needed to start being very explicit about our expected norms and behavior in our school, then to identify particular skills around social and civic behavior that we wanted the kids to have. We had to decide as a faculty how to respond when kids violated those civic expectations in a way that also supported them. Consistency was important, and we hoped to have all of the adults in a student's life, using the same language to reinforce positive behavior.

An effective school community, we needed to answer the question: how will we keep growing? I identified external measures as a reason for growth. There were things we could work on within the school, but out there, outside the school, there are some real issues. We were having conversations and making team-based decisions around how to get our kids ready for that. At that point we were really at the beginning and hadn't solved everything. We recognized that it was continuous work. The key was learning how to share your message so that people understood it.

Leadership Roles: Principal, Staff, Teachers

I understood the passion that people in the community had and realized that they needed to see a leader taking charge. I really needed to figure out what that meant.

It started by being visible and communicating. The school community politics, the parent politics, the diversity of the city—you have to keep in touch with that and you have to keep communicating. In such a large school, making sure that the teachers as well as the superintendent are aware of what's going on is essential. Communication at every level is important.

This job creates tension between wanting to feel like you're a part of the community and recognizing that you have a level of authority. If you put too much emphasis on authority, then you're disconnected, but becoming too connected can cause a loss in authority. As a principal, I've tried to find that balance.

With longer-term decisions, you want to avoid having a top-down process—it should be inclusive. For example, after the flag incident, we defused the immediate tension and could then step out of crisis mode and reflect on where we were. As a result I created that student-faculty group. I'm a strong believer in distributing leadership and empowering others. A lot of people are more comfortable having someone else—the principal—make decisions; then there is someone to blame if things go wrong. But a distribution of leadership and power is a foundation for a strong school culture. And that's something that's very good at Newton North.

My administrative team was leading the charge in determining where the school was heading instructionally and how we would achieve our goals. I met with the whole team weekly: department heads, deans, and my vice principals. We formed a collaborative problem-solving group. It wasn't a "Henry-runs-the-meeting" kind of situation. Everyone had a voice.

I was getting feedback that people who never thought they could take on leadership roles were doing so. It wasn't just the same old guard speaking in faculty meetings. We created assistant department head roles focused on managing the MCAS in each department, and some of our newer teachers stepped up into those positions. I think that empowered others and helped move the school in a good direction. That was exciting.

REFLECTIONS

What helped me be a successful leader at Newton North was coming into the school at a time where their need matched my leadership philosophy and style. I believe in distributed leadership: empowering people to take on leadership roles within the school community. Being an experienced principal paid off because I had learned a lot about myself already. I knew I was capable of fostering strong relationships; people knew that I cared about them.

My leadership is transitioning from needing to continuously remind folks to take leadership initiative to supporting them in doing this. Now they have bought into it. We just had our annual winter retreat in January, and there was resounding support for the vision of the school.

They are seeing the school's vision as their personal vision and owning the schoolwide vision. A lot of the work has been focused on talking about instruction and shifting to teaching that is more student-centered and differentiated. There are resistors and people who are just starting the work, but there is a strong energy among my 17-person leadership team that wasn't there two years ago. We have been able to maintain our culture as one where we take care of each other which has helped us get through some of those challenges.

Feedback is one way that I'm checking my barometers: Am I too far ahead? Too far behind? I have been focusing and working with how we handle the feedback we are getting. Staff felt there was no structure for them to share feedback. The feedback was tied to culture as well. Folks want more opportunities to provide administrators with feedback about the school climate and the work we are doing. From the admin point of view, collecting feedback is helpful for understanding where people stand in terms of the work they wanted to do; the shifts and changes they wanted.

We heard from staff that they felt we needed to improve the way they could share feedback. They wanted it to be actionable so that the person would receive the feedback and change their practice. My administrators are now really buying into the work. They see the benefit of it as opposed to being fearful. They realize this is actually going to help them see the current reality on where people stand.

LOOKING FORWARD

A theme of this past year's community work is that less is more. We are focusing on the essential work, but also not feeling pressured to work 24/7. That message has gone a long way to help people recognize that we know people have complicated lives outside of their work and we want them feeling rested and fresh when they are working with the kids. We are trying to pay attention to how to support people who are going through hard times. It's something we are trying to model and emphasize.

I feel we are in a very good place as a school. I'm energized by the continuous work we are doing. Our lens for the foreseeable future is to focus on instruction and shift our classrooms to be more student-centered. We want students to be problem solving and collaborating through a variety of culturally responsive instructional practices offered. Changing our instructional practices is our way of closing the achievement gap. This year, we have had three professional days where we focused on teachers trying something new in their work with students: identifying a skill that they wanted students to develop.

We have also been learning about culturally responsive instruction, which is tied to understanding the cultural differences of students and supporting their needs in an instructional environment. Students of color have shared with teachers about what works best in the classroom for students of color. We have a speaker who is going to talk about the concept of how to be both an empathetic teacher and one who expects a lot from students. Teachers are very engaged. Some have run with it while others have slowly been getting on board. The fact that we are doing this work, and the administrators are not only supporting it on professional days but supporting it in their departmental work, is really exciting and lays the foundation for where we will be going in the next couple of years. It works around a couple structural changes: (1) Students have more access to laptops at school now. Three-quarters of students have chrome books. (2) There has been a lot of talk about a possible new schedule, which could be a huge shift for our school. Two constructs: one is longer teaching instructional blocks, the other is a flex block to give students a time to get help from teachers, get homework done, or do enrichment to address some of the mental health challenges. Those two concepts tie into the need to shift our instructional practices. I'm very excited about it.

My mission is to shift our instructional practices so that students are developing skills that are much more applicable to what the future expects of them. Students are learning how to learn, not necessarily learning content. The superintendent is with me and so is my direct supervisor, who is the assistant superintendent for secondary schools. There is a lot of work to do but we have come a long way.

I'd like to see us get to a place where we have clear goals for student outcomes, including goals for their civic skill development, mental/

emotional support, and anti-bias work. All of those things point to student outcomes: How are students doing?

Our work has shifted from being MCAS-focused to being centered around helping students develop through our anti bias curriculum and social-emotional learning curriculums and, of course, supporting students when they struggle. We have been doing well on MCAS scores, but our outcomes should also be measured by the diversity in our upper-level classes. We're finding that African American students, for example, are underrepresented. So, progress in those areas is how I define success. Right now, that's where we are focusing our efforts

Henry balanced the strength of his personal relationships with faculty and his role as the leader of Bedford and Newton North High Schools enabling people to take ownership of the teaching and learning in the schools. At entry to both, he interviewed and had personal trust-building conversations with as many teachers and administrators who would accept his invitation. In both schools, the vast majority responded positively. Henry made himself personally accessible as he reached out to the full faculty, an ambitious aspiration for both schools with faculty sizes in the hundreds. By establishing individual trusting relationships early in his tenure, he facilitated change through his department leaders in response to the needs of each school.

In both schools, Henry's leadership provided autonomy for teachers. By offering autonomy to the leadership team, he inspired them to actively lead their departments and work together. At Bedford High School Henry invigorated the Program Administrators by giving them autonomy over their sessions and trusted them to resolve the iPad issue while remaining available for support. The Program Administrators became change agents as they worked with the entire faculty. Additionally, Henry enabled teachers to take ownership for planning and instructing the Ed Camp sessions. The professional learning of Ed Camp was the ultimate measure of teacher-directed learning with one another.

Henry translated a racist and politically biased incident that occurred at Newton North during the start of the school year into a focal point for faculty and student collaboration. Henry used the incident to involve both teachers and students in the response. A group of students were ready to protest the parade of cars carrying Confederate flags with a walkout and demonstration outside the school. Henry met with the students to redirect their passion and maintain student safety. He was able to divert the possibility of physical injury that could occur during a protest outside by partnering with students to organize a whole school rally on social justice and anti-racism. Their in-school protest was highly visible, well attended and peaceful. The rally stimulated many students and teachers to initiate a more active role in social justice and anti-racism. Henry fostered this commitment by creating a committee that included students and faculty who were passionate about an anti-bias curriculum at the school. The committee worked to develop and put in place a curriculum throughout a building of over 2,000 high school students.

Henry's leadership is built on developing a relationship of mutual trust with his faculty members. He serves as a coalescing agent, bringing faculty together for heightened student learning. In both high schools, he has brought about positive change in the ways his faculty work together to solve the thorny issues they confront. He continues to build a vision for Newton North that includes greater participation in upper level courses by minority students, enhanced social/emotional wellbeing of students and increased understanding of culturally responsive teaching by the faculty.

4

Beth Ludwig

Lincoln Street Elementary School

2009-2011

Hanscom Primary School

2011-2019

Leadership Story

I STARTED MY TEACHING career spending four years as a reading specialist and assistant to the principal in Wakefield, Massachusetts. I then transitioned to a reading specialist and literacy coach position at Hanscom Primary School, located on the Hanscom Air Force Base in Massachusetts. After five years there and graduating from the Educator Leadership Institute, I left Hanscom Primary to pursue my first elementary principalship at Lincoln Street School in Northborough, Massachusetts.

First Lessons–Lincoln Street School

Lincoln Street School had about 500 students from kindergarten through fifth grade. At 32 years old, I was one of the youngest people in the school—and the building leader. Early on, I often questioned my capacity to provide feedback and recommendations that would be respected. As I began building relationships, this feeling dissipated but never fully disappeared. For reasons I still cannot identify precisely, I felt that even positive feedback would feel condescending coming from a young leader. It was my own personal struggle, resolved only with time and experience.

Reflecting on the feedback from faculty during my entry interviews, I concluded that although my predecessor had strengths, she hadn't made instructional leadership her primary focus. I had confidence I had much to offer in that regard. As a novice in other areas, the leadership learning curve was steep in the first two years. I had to learn quickly how to cope with some challenging faculty members and families, a highly involved parent population, and entering a school with very few structures in place (general organization, discipline, and consistent curriculum and learning outcomes). In those first years, it was easy to take things personally, and I had to learn that the actions of some were not a reflection of me but rather systems that had been built into the culture over time. It was necessary for me to respond to an array of personalities with strength, but also with compassion and support.

Despite initial challenges, most faculty members demonstrated eagerness, excitement, and commitment to improving teaching and learning. This allowed for some highly engaging exchanges with people who walked away genuinely wanting to put new ideas into action. I felt an overwhelming sense of support from faculty and eventually, the parent community. They were invested in me and my success and went out of their way to offer encouragement and support.

DEALING WITH A SCHOOL CRISIS

During my first week at Lincoln Street School, a student who had been battling cancer passed away. I walked into an emotional and challenging situation. I grieved with my new school community and surely felt the gravity of this great loss.

I had to learn very quickly how to manage a very complex and urgent situation. I called the crisis team together and was surprised to learn that it consisted of 15 people. It was far too large and included many people with emotions and experiences connected to the student. I knew I had to reduce the size of the crisis team. I explained to them that in order to best address the needs of the school community and the student's family, the team's size would be reduced. Even in the smaller team, emotionally charged conversations ensued.

The crisis team was responsible for addressing communications with the community and managing feedback regarding how best to pay tribute to this student. My challenge was making sure the whole school community was heard and represented, while being clear that the final decisions would be made by the student's family and me. I'd never interacted directly with the student's parents, but I reached out to collaborate on the manner in which they wanted him remembered at the school. That felt monumental; I was as new to the family as they were to me. I needed to be my best, most authentic self. Upon reflection, I feel positive about how we worked together. Our ongoing communication led to the tribute they imagined. I felt I had successfully done what was needed for the school and community at the time. Regardless, at the end of the day a student's life had ended and that tragedy would never escape me.

EARLY CHANGES: GRABBING THE LOW-HANGING FRUIT

We often talk about "grabbing the low-hanging fruit" the first year. I was committed to taking actions that were high priority for faculty and families that did not reach far into instructional practice or community traditions. The information gained from entry interviews was key in identifying these priorities. For faculty, unclear discipline policy and procedures rose to the top while families were concerned with improving instruction, leadership, and parking lot safety. That year, I worked with faculty to design a student-friendly "Citizenship Agreement" that articulated community values and school rules. It also created a specific discipline protocol based on progressive discipline approaches. The agreement gave students, teachers, and families a clear understanding of our school values and behavioral expectations. I saw this agreement as a positive early win. It helped the faculty see my willingness to listen and provide collaborative, actionable results.

In that first year, I believe I was able to extend my reach beyond the low-hanging fruit because of the faculty's energy and openness. I advocated for funding, developed a leveled literacy library, and with the help of faculty got it up and running. I was able to start talking about twenty-first-century learning skills by incorporating shared readings into faculty and school site council meetings that included parents and teachers in the same group. This contributed to the design of our mission and vision statement and school improvement goals. It was exciting and enriching. Overall, I remain incredibly grateful for my time at Lincoln Street School. The faculty and staff were some of the finest, most dedicated educators I will ever know. And the community, which I grew to love, was remarkably invested in the education of their students.

Returning to Hanscom Primary School (HPS)

Hanscom Primary School (HPS), while situated on the Air Force Base, was part of the Lincoln Public Schools in Lincoln, Massachusetts. The school was my professional home; I've always loved it. I had been a literacy specialist for five years prior and a literacy coach for three years, and I maintained a wonderful relationship with many former colleagues, including my predecessor. It was always in my mind's eye to return to Hanscom, so when my predecessor retired, there was minimal hesitation before I applied for the principalship. I do recall, however, experiencing emotions to an unanticipated degree. I'd grown very attached to Lincoln Street School—the faculty, students, families, and my principal colleagues. It was a comfortable environment where great things were taking off and, in hindsight, it was a really terrific role. I felt more conflicted than I imagined. When I became a finalist for the Hanscom position, I remember sharing the news with faculty and feeling the guilt of potentially leaving a school that respected, trusted, and depended on me. The decision to leave Lincoln Street was undeniably hard, but I moved forward knowing I would grow as a result.

Old Politics and Internal Opposition

Returning to your "home school" as prospective principal is one of the most challenging ways to attain and be successful in the job. Some of my previous professional audacity haunted me in this process. There was expected fear of change, but also the reputation I had built. I was known to push teachers to achieve more for students. This concerned some faculty, and to be fair, their concerns were based in reality. I do not suggest that they were averse to change, but perhaps more fearful of the unknown being forced upon them too quickly. This reluctance caused me to wonder if I would get the job.

Nevertheless, the finalist process continued, and a committee from Hanscom conducted a site visit at Lincoln Street. I was allowed to select the people and groups with whom they met (which included teachers, administrators, students, and parents). I intentionally took a risk and chose a unique K–5 student cohort—some of whom may not have painted the rosiest picture of me. I wanted the group to reflect an array of individual experiences with me. It was a risk worth taking. Ultimately, this group and others began to solidify my candidacy in the minds of those on the hiring committee.

I learned that details carry significant weight during an interview process. When students honestly shared their unique experiences, it helped the hiring committee see the relationships I had built with a variety of students and that students came first. Arranging meetings with all stakeholders (faculty, families, and administrative colleagues) allowed me to demonstrate the breadth of my collaborative work. My final part of the interview at Hanscom Primary was an open forum with families. As I was waiting in the lobby, some students were waiting for their parents with little to do. Instinctively, I sat down and engaged in conversation. After being hired I learned that for many parents attending this forum, observing this interaction is what mattered most to them. I learned that both as a candidate or principal, everyone is constantly paying attention to every move you make. Even the smallest moments are an expression of who you are and contribute to people's opinions about you. These small things, as well as my proven ability to manage and provide instructional leadership, are what landed me the job. Throughout this process and beyond, I had a mentor of mine whispering his mantra in my ear: "I run for principal every day."

Challenges of Identity

One of the first things that weighed heavily on my mind was assimilating with a mostly conservative military community as an openly gay principal. It was during that same year that the federal "Don't ask, don't tell" policy was repealed. Still, some more conservative families had inquiries about "the Massachusetts agenda" (referring to state liberals pushing values that could affect our instructional design).

My wife was pregnant with our first child at the time and her due date was September 10—during the second week of school. This was a big challenge just starting out. I was not willing to hide who I was; I had to continue being my authentic self. Pragmatically, I also had a child coming, and knew that I had to take at least a week off. I distinctly remember holding my son in the hospital with one arm and my laptop with the other. Leading crucial early-year/entry faculty meetings weighed heavily on my mind.

All at once, my first child was born, I was beginning a new job, and I had to make the community aware of my absence (which involved coming out all over again on a very broad scale). Before school began, I wrote a letter to the community disclosing my sexual orientation and the imminent arrival of our son. It was a lot, but I had to believe most families would understand and welcome me as they would any new member of the community. And they did. In retrospect, I am sad to have only taken one week for my wife and child. It was hard, but when you are a principal, duty is always calling. You need to understand and respect the enormity of the job and the sacrifices demanded of you.

I ripped off a few band-aids at once those first few weeks of school, which ended up being a positive thing. I am grateful that the world has changed drastically since 2011. I never would have expected it, but the base now recognizes Pride Week each April. There have been some minor bruises along the way prompted by some parents' perceptions of having a gay principal, but nothing hugely significant ever occurred. I believe this in part because people's perspectives are evolving, and in part because I worked hard to build relationships with families early. It was important that families grew to know the person I am, respect my leadership, and have faith that their students were in exceptional hands during the school day.

Hanscom Entry Plan

My challenge coming to Hanscom was very different than it had been during my first principal experience at Lincoln Street. My role there had been providing instructional leadership and capitalizing on faculty energy for change. It was relatively easy to move the faculty who, overall, were hungry for change and improvement. My role and challenge at Hanscom was how to take a high-functioning group of self-starters, move them forward, and further evolve their professional practice. They were more accustomed to researching and implementing bold ideas on their own rather than being led toward a specific idea or instructional concept that would influence student learning.

It takes a unique group of educators to work in a military setting and my 75-person staff was no exception. You have got to be ready and willing to hit the ground running with students who arrive from all over the world at any given time during the school year and bring a range of academic, social, emotional, and behavioral skill sets. You need to be nimble. There is a collective understanding that time with students is precious and that, during that time, everyone must do everything in their power to help each student grow. There is a lot of pride in serving military students and their families.

Before school started in September, I invited faculty to spend an hour one-on-one with me. That was the first layer of discovery. My questions ranged from instruction to culture: What would they like to see? What do they celebrate? What do they wish to continue? Do we function as a team or as individuals? What has the school done to build educator capacity? These opening conversations were helpful to me and to the faculty. Communicating my interest in learning multiple perspectives was essential in building trust with the faculty.

When the school year began, I chose to focus primarily on building relationships and working to further uncover the areas for improvement identified by faculty. I grew to further learn of people's readiness for small, incremental change. Overall however, the mentality appeared to be, "We're pretty great as we are." In some ways this was true, but there is always room for growth. Helping them to see this became an important priority.

It is not possible to be an influencer without building mutual trust; my first year was about developing trusting relationships and letting the school community get to know me as a leader. This meant ongoing communication, modeling expectations, ensuring they had the resources necessary for instruction, and constantly communicating my fundamental core value of focusing on student learning. "How will your plan or idea impact student learning?" became a question they learned to expect.

The arrival of my first child helped reveal, in part, the person I am. My son's birth provided unexpected solidarity with teachers. Whether they were parents or not, there was a feeling of connection. They appreciated and recognized I could offer compassion if they were having a family situation. I could be flexible and say, "You've got to miss the faculty meeting. So what? Family first." That was my message from the beginning. They saw it, and it was valued.

EXTERNAL MANDATES FOR CHANGE

This time period also coincided with the first years of the new State Educator Evaluation System, which I supported since its launch. A new evaluation system coupled with experiencing it with a new principal created understandable anxiety. To minimize this, I repeated the points: "I'm learning this with you, I am working with the district to make this process as clear as possible, I view myself as co-planner and coach in the process." It was good for the faculty to see me as a person willing to wrestle through some tricky instructional decisions with them. I repeated often, especially with new teachers, "If any part of this lesson fails, we both own it. We will reflect and make improvements for the next lesson together."

As year one progressed, questions about student learning began to emerge, some of which included: Do students understand what they are learning about and why? Do they know the criteria for success in the classroom? Are kids engaged in meaningful learning experiences? Is the learning environment safe, supportive, and well managed? Is it student-centered? Is it collaborative, or are our students working mostly independently? Are there solid routines in place?

I shared my evolving questions in faculty meetings, being careful not to overwhelm. The group I led tended to dissect most communications by me, sometimes resulting in clarity, other times in misunderstanding. Some faculty's protective impulse was to become worried and defensive. They felt that raising the questions implied I was not observing any of these elements in their instruction. In reality, I was aiming for consistency and depth.

Overall, anonymous faculty feedback from my first year was very positive. I believe most were pleasantly surprised that I did not move forward with any big action steps. Not pushing your program right away is very often a good thing. Waiting to implement change is not always comfortable, but it's critical. In the first year, it took a lot of restraint for me to not aim higher than the low-hanging frut.

COMMUNITY OUTREACH

Hanscom Primary School consists of about 320 students preK–3, while Hanscom Middle School serves grades 4–8. Hanscom schools are one of only three school systems in the country that are located on military bases but function as public schools. The facilities, however, are owned and funded by a contract with the Department of Defense.

Every two to three years, the district must reapply for the contract through the Department of Defense. If we were to ever lose that contract, it would leave the employment of many Hanscom faculty and administrators at high risk. Therefore, I took my responsibility seriously to continuously highlight and celebrate the distinctive role of our school in the community. This in effect, put me in the role of school-based public relations manager. At times, this "PR Manager" role involved interacting with federal representatives in Congress. An ongoing priority was to be certain that leadership at all levels was well connected to our success.

BEHAVIORAL, EMOTIONAL, SOCIAL SUPPORT TEAM (BESST)

Student behavior was another focus during my first year (and beyond). During entry interviews, observations, and conversations with faculty, I understood the urgency. Like many public schools, we were dealing with many significant mental health, social-emotional, and behavioral challenges with students. We were observing behaviors we had never before experienced; students behaving dangerously and faculty having to do more de-escalations, escorts, and mild restraints as a result. The actions and behaviors of some students were impacting the learning of others. The faculty and I were spending more time responding to student behavior, and I was dedicating most of my time to working with these students and de-escalating parent concerns. What made our situation unique was not only the high rate of aggressive behavior, extreme noncompliance, and rates of student and family trauma, but also the lack of personnel and programmatic resources to adequately address the situations. Due to the small size of the preK–8 district, we lacked the appropriate program for students with social-emotional and/or behavioral skill deficits. The district was spending an average of $800,000 a year on outside placements. It seemed that no matter what protocols we had in place; we were often reacting instead of being proactive. The school already had very thorough discipline protocols. The question became, "How do we best meet the needs of students who are socially, emotionally, and/or behaviorally at risk?"

I knew students and teachers needed support. I had done a fair amount of research on Positive Behavior Intervention Systems (PBIS). We received district funding to focus three summer days to address this dilemma. At that point, I was really learning how to design effective, outcome-based, collaborative meetings. As the facilitator, I dedicated much time to selecting the appropriate articles to build background knowledge, designing a meeting structure that allowed for maximum participation and input, and writing focused guiding questions. At the beginning of the workshop, the team collaboratively listed desired outcomes.

We had terrific representation at the table. I prepared readings on PBIS research and connections to response to intervention (RTI). Our work resulted in the establishment of a Behavioral, Emotional, Social Support Team (BESST). Its function is similar to a student study team with primary focus on students with social-emotional and/or behavioral skill deficits.

That summer, the team developed a community resource by merging our Student Code of Conduct with information about PBIS and

BESST. We developed a mission and vision for social- emotional and behavioral prerequisites for learning, defined the role of each BESST team member, and created meeting norms, protocols, and guiding questions. We updated our "Citizenship Agreement" (kid-friendly school rules) to include specific criteria for success in each school setting. We also agreed to begin collecting and tracking discipline data. The team left the summer work exhausted—but exhilarated. Reflecting on what we accomplished in three days still amazes me. The entire team presented the work to faculty. Teachers felt heard and saw the actionable response. It was a huge win for faculty and students.

Over the years, after gathering schoolwide feedback, the BESST model evolved and improved. Ultimately, it became a district model. The data collected over time helped to present a compelling case to district administrators and the school committee for increased resources. This small shift eventually resulted in the hiring of a full-time K–8 behavior consultant/behavior analyst (BCBA) at Hanscom, the addition of one school psychologist for each building: the primary and middle schools (they had previously shared one), and eventually, in the new school facility, a K–5 therapeutic intervention program (with a lead teacher/instructional coach and tutor). At-risk students could be temporarily placed in this setting, and the lead teacher could push into classrooms to support students and offer coaching to classroom teachers.

UNIQUE CHALLENGES WITH A TRANSIENT POPULATION

At Hanscom, due to our transient military population, the preK–8 schools turn over one-third of the student population annually. While the bulk of our students transition over the summer, many students transition in and out of the school throughout the year. It is not uncommon for each classroom teacher to have six or seven students joining and leaving their class during the year. Students come from all over the country and the world, highlighting the educational disparities in our country and a unique gap in educational opportunities.

When family members deploy and return home, there is often a dramatic impact at home. There is fear, anxiety, change in parenting structure, hidden effects, and at times, trauma. The school has to be prepared to support students and families through these transitions. The faculty at Hanscom excel at managing these transitions.

Our student population is enriched with racial, ethnic, religious, regional, and gender diversity. We also have a small community of English language learners. We celebrate this and also recognize the immense responsibility we have to provide an outstanding education that meets the needs of each learner.

IMPROVING THE EDUCATIONAL EXPERIENCE FOR ALL LEARNERS

Heading into my second year at HPS, the middle school principal and I took bold, collaborative action. We embarked on a multi-year professional development and improvement plan to influence instructional practice—not *what* students learned but how they learned it. We used the shared text *Learning Targets: Helping Students Aim for Understanding in Today's Lesson* (Moss and Brookhart, 2012) and aligned professional development to lay the framework for using the formative learning cycle (FLC) across K–8 instruction. The FLC connects a learning target to the criteria for success for meeting the target (both written in student-friendly language) using a strong performance- based learning activity that produces evidence of students' progress toward the learning target. The FLC also allows for student goal-setting, assessments directly linked to learning targets and criteria for success, and a continuous feedback loop (teacher-to-student and student-to-student).

We wanted to teach faculty each aspect of the FLC in depth, allow time for practice, and create a professional learning program that continuously built on the teachers' knowledge and experiences. Our expectation was that all faculty would gradually implement each aspect of the FLC after learning each new concept, which took about one year per concept. We allowed time for collaboration and discussion. Each year of professional development yielded positive results. Inconsistencies in application existed, but we worked closely with individual teachers who struggled. The district would adopt a similar model and provide resources to support more involved professional development and district goals using the book *Leaders of Their Own Learning: Transforming Schools Through Student-Engaged Assessment* (Berger and Rugen, 2014) as the foundational common reading. District focus helped reignite areas where practice had weakened over time.

This was an experience in taking audacious, student-centered action relatively early on. Although at times it was flawed and imprecise, it was ultimately a necessary and successful step forward in establishing a consistent, deeper learning experience for all students. The tightening of learning goals and the precision of language required deep introspection on the part of faculty. It also helped two principals collaboratively reflect, respond, change course, and listen more closely to students and teachers.

THE DILEMMA—LEARNING GAPS

When a school turns over one-third of its population each year, this means that very few students begin in kindergarten and matriculate through third grade. This can result in significant learning gaps. The Lincoln School District and Hanscom Schools dedicated significant time, resources, and professional development to balanced literacy practices and as a result, changed many teachers' perspective on quality literacy instruction. In December, the third-grade team requested my presence at a team meeting, sharing honestly their concerns that most students were not receiving daily small group reading instruction. The range of readers' levels in each classroom was broad and unmanageable (ranging from grades 1 to 5). It was impossible to provide whole class instruction while adequately targeting the instruction for many small groups within the literacy block. Ultimately, they were seeking a solution that met the needs of all readers in third grade and believed they had exhausted all possibilities. The literacy coach and I viewed this as a more complex, schoolwide dilemma and welcomed this as an opportunity for transformational change. This was not merely a "third-grade problem" to resolve; all grade-level teams were facing similar instructional challenges and could perhaps benefit from this same discussion.

I had the support of an extremely talented literacy coach who had built meaningful and trusting relationships with teams. Together (with the support of the Superintendent and District Content Specialist) we strategized next steps for this team and the school. To begin, we reviewed the fall third-grade Fountas and Pinnell Benchmark Assessment System

(BAS) data. Forty-three percent of the students fell into the extreme high-risk and high-risk bands on the BAS. All students in these bands were on IEPs. Thirty-two percent of students began the year on benchmark while 25 percent exceeded benchmark. One of the most striking data points was that we were effectively meeting the needs of 57 percent of the cohort. Grades 1 and 2 revealed similar trends. Because third-grade teachers had raised the issue, our plan was to begin this work with them before moving on to preceding grades.

THE PILOT

After a daylong collaborative practice meeting with the third-grade team, we agreed to take some dramatic steps to improve the effectiveness and efficiency of instruction during the literacy block. During their literacy block, we would dedicate all available teaching resources to small group, differentiated reading. The literacy coach would train the classroom assistants and special education support staff in intervention strategies. All educators would accept and share responsibility for *all* grade 3 students.

We dissolved the self-contained classroom model during small group reading time. Flexible groups were created by using reading levels and performance bands to determine cohort groupings. During the literacy block, many students would move to a different classroom, rotating through targeted "stations" led by an adult. We shifted our approach from relying solely on benchmark outcomes to developing and monitoring individualized student growth goals. To avoid perceptions or feelings of the old "tracking" model, we were sure to create a structure where students could move between groups (at any time) based on their performance.

RESULTS

The pilot allowed us to reduce the range of readers in a classroom. Teachers had time to work with all reading levels every single day. Ultimately, between January and May we were able to celebrate some striking results; 85 percent of third grade students met, exceeded, or were on track to meet individual growth goals by the end of the school year.

After this rather aggressive mid-year change, we were effectively meeting the needs of 84 percent of students, which was a dramatic change from the 57 percent in December. And the feedback from students was completely positive. Many expressed their desire to continue this model in fourth grade.

The results of this work informed some school improvement efforts for years to come. The literacy coach worked with K–3 teams to develop grade-level growth rate expectations, monitor students, and design targeted instruction. Faculty deepened their shared understanding of the elements of high-quality, balanced, targeted, and differentiated small group reading instruction. This led to more masterful planning and teaching of small, flexible groups of readers.

THE NEW BUILDING: DESIGNING A COLLABORATIVE SHARED VISION

Having a strong, clear vision for the future of my school community has been a foundational strength I continue to hone. As a new principal, I had viewed my role as "selling" my vision to faculty. Over time, I grew to understand that my ability to design a collaborative vision would be the most valuable and sustainable course of action. Designing a new state-of-the-art learning facility presented a unique opportunity to craft a collaborative shared vision and imagine new possibilities for teaching and learning in the new space. Energy and enthusiasm were in place! Then came the unexpected.

PERSONAL HEALTH CRISIS

Three years into my time at HPS, I was formally diagnosed with dystonia, a neurological movement disorder that causes intermittent muscle contractions resulting in involuntary, restless movements. There is no cure, only treatment. Dystonia does not have a cognitive impact, only physical. The onset of my symptoms started ten years prior; after my first year in the principalship. At that time, I noticed some clenching and slight involuntary movement in my right hand. It progressed slowly into my right arm and shoulder and became more pronounced. For several years, it did not hugely impact my work or life.

My symptoms were mostly subtle and functional until about six years into my principalship at HPS. Then I noticed my eyes began to twitch and spasm; I paid it no attention at the time. That September, at the district's first administrative council meeting, the movements in my hand and arm became significant. When tasked with reading through the teachers' contract, I suddenly felt my eyes lock in a closed position. I couldn't read the words on the page. It scared me beyond belief. As I was excused from the meeting, I found myself asking, "Will I be okay? What does this mean for my work? For my family?" I had experienced moments in my life where it felt like everything was crashing down on me; and this time, it really was. As the first month of school moved along, my symptoms grew increasingly worse. My eyes were spasming and closing so frequently I had trouble reading, typing, walking, and driving. My right hand and arm were in constant involuntary motion. At the end of September that year, I began a medical leave of absence.

My primary goal was to return to work, so during my leave I focused on trying every possible kind of therapy and treatment to regain function. There was not a strategy I was unwilling to try. My life became completely focused on a balance between neuroplastic exercises to retrain my brain and giving my body the rest it so desperately needed due to the high energy output of intense movements. I did physical therapy, Qi Gong, and meditation and mindfulness work. I began running to improve my vision and balance. I spent over a year with a psychiatrist participating in cognitive behavioral therapy, an approach that helps you become aware of inaccurate or negative thinking so you can view challenging situations more clearly and respond to them in a more effective way. I saw multiple neurologists, who responded with treatments from Botox injections to Parkinson's medications.

After nearly one year of leave, I felt confident that I had my symptoms under control. I was in a really good place and feeling very prepared to return to work that July. I knew it would be hard; the job is hard if you are the healthiest person on the planet, but I have never been one to give up. Even with my symptoms, I said to myself, "There are many people with a plethora of disabilities who do this job—and others—and they persevere and so will I."

Returning After Leave

The reentry process was more challenging than I expected. During my leave, the Interim Principal was successful in her role of maintaining the school and continuing some work on the shared vision. She developed strong relationships with some faculty. Upon my return, there were some faculty members who I had hired just prior to my leave; and I hadn't had the opportunity to build relationships with them. I felt a hesitancy on the part of faculty and administrative colleagues and sensed I had something to prove. They viewed me as fragile. With the best of intentions, they were worried about me. I did my best to reassure them and provide confidence in my leadership. I also resurfaced vulnerability with a fresh perspective, sharing with them how my journey influenced me as a person and leader. I promised they would experience a "tamer" version of the "old Beth." Despite this, I could still sense the trepidation. Words could not compensate for time apart; only actions could.

I began my re-entry that summer by meeting with all central office administrators, other principals, the literacy and math coach, and the social worker. I also held work sessions with two groups: team leaders and new and "new-ish" faculty. For new-ish faculty, I designed a half-day workshop aimed at relationship building through sharing personal and professional core values that impact our work and life.

There was much to revisit and unpack: What had happened since I left? How will I address the chronic problems that plagued previous shared vision faculty meetings? This was my problem—I owned it and knew that this was my one shot at a "do-over." I wanted to see faculty more actively engaged; I wanted less eyes glazing over and more enthusiasm, fun, laughter, humor, and multi layered, meaningful exchange. I wanted everyone to feel safe to be vulnerable, authentic, and share openly and honestly. Even though some business about transitioning to a new facility was necessary, I wanted faculty to feel that it was their time, not solely mine. It was time to address things differently, giving them insight into the "new Beth."

SYSTEMS THINKING

"Systems thinking" is a business model focused on collaborative protocols and formulas for change. Systems thinking helps people view systems from a broad perspective. It includes identifying overall structures, patterns, and cycles in a system rather than only seeing individual events in the system. I used systems thinking with team leaders to bring new life to the shared vision discussion. I wanted to create a workshop that was engaging, honest, and fully collaborative. This model fit because it required the curiosity, clarity, compassion, choice, and courage I wanted to model and teachers to experience.

I selected systems thinking because I viewed it as a relatively low-stakes strategy to acquire the most honest feedback necessary that would improve our shared vision process. I was both a facilitator and a participant in this process. Systems thinking asked team leaders to move from participating in and observing events at previous shared vision faculty meetings to helping me identify patterns of positive, productive, unproductive, and/or restrictive actions that took place at those meetings. Through this process, we surfaced successful meeting structures and underlying problems in previous shared vision meetings. As a result, we created a more satisfying long-term solution for all.

At the request of team leaders, the focus of future shared vision meetings would shift away from full-faculty editing and revision of the shared vision statement. Instead, team leaders and I would work to create a more concise document that would be presented to faculty for feedback and consensus vote.

We agreed we wanted the "mood" of team leaders' meetings to be positive, engaging, and fun. I asked the team to make a promise: I wanted them to notify me *during* meetings if things were not going as planned or needed changing. I wanted feedback in the moment rather than hearing months later how things could have been better. I wanted their help in noticing and making flexible adjustments mid meeting. Initially, this was met with wild-eyed silence. Eventually some asked, "Are you sure you mean that, Beth? That feels hard. We know how hard you plan for those meetings and you have everything planned so efficiently that it's hard to disrupt."

I appreciated the recognition of the effort I put into planning meetings, but realized I had been overplanning meetings to the point of inflexibility. I needed to rethink how I ran meetings. I recall saying, "I've always asked teachers to respond to the needs of the students in front of them. I must expect the same of myself and provide more flexibility based on my observations of adults." Hearing this from me seemed to provide staff with more confidence in me. I would make significant efforts to improve shared vision meetings after receiving this feedback.

We shared the conversations we had during team leaders' meetings with the rest of the faculty that fall. We were making the collective statement that faculty was being trusted as a collaborative group to decide what was most important to them in terms of the shared vision. Teachers saw that they were going to have a choice in how to use their meeting time; their voices were being heard. This was a significant step in moving our shared vision process forward. It was also a huge lesson in responsive, corrective leadership. It demonstrated to me that there is much to be learned when we collaborate, reflect honesty, and seek out advice and support from teachers.

New Perspective, Same Beliefs

Around November of that year, I could feel the dystonia symptoms returning. They increased rapidly and with greater intensity, and just before December recess, I took a leave from my role at Hanscom Primary School. I resigned from my position a month later. It was a heartbreaking separation for me; I grieved the loss of purpose, community, and camaraderie my job had brought me. Resigning, however, was necessary and in the best interest of the school, my family, and me.

Soon after my resignation, I lost complete motor control of all upper extremities—my hands, arms, eyes, face, jaw, head, neck, and diaphragm. In June, I underwent deep brain stimulation (DBS). A neurosurgical device was implanted in my brain; it is most commonly used to treat Parkinson's. I can report happily that by that December, some of my most severe symptoms began to abate.

I have no regrets about my attempt to return to Hanscom. At the time, I was ready, but after six months, my body was sending me a different message. During my first medical leave, my determination and perseverance to control my health stemmed from a desire to return to work. Perhaps that was part noble and part selfish, as working in Lincoln and at HPS meant so much to me. After experiencing what I had gone through, I learned that my truest, boldest purpose was regaining health for me, my family, and my friends. Dystonia and the job took precious moments from me. I now have a chance to live a great life again, filled with joy and gratitude.

REFLECTIONS

When one school committee member described me as "bold, brave, and never afraid," I was flattered—I'd always aspired to be those things. But embracing vulnerability has always been a focus in our school. I believe there is power in modeling this for students and adults. I want students and teachers to allow themselves to be vulnerable in a trusting environment so they can take risks and find comfort in learning from failure. Creating a culture where these actions and mindset are pervasive has been some of the most challenging and rewarding work.

I'm a believer in the power of strong school leadership. The lessons learned will carry me far into my life and future careers. I will never stop being an audacious, courageous, risk-taking leader—or person. I am eternally grateful for every person I have met along the way; from each, there was a story and lesson learned. I will never underestimate the personal and professional value of being an active observer, participant, listener, and learner. And we did, in the end, help construct the most amazing elementary learning facility I have ever seen.

This job is incredibly hard, unbelievably demanding, and undeniably taxing. You have to be simultaneously audacious, fair, thick-skinned, kind, vulnerable, and strong. The demands placed upon you shift from moment to moment. This requires flexibility, patience, and a growth mindset. You have got to be confident in and comfortable with who you are. At your core, you have to be a good person with positive intentions, attitude, agency, and solid values. It will all be called into question, doubted, and misunderstood at times, but you have to have a strong moral compass pulling you through such moments. The work has taught me that I have much strength and courage.

PARTING RECOMMENDATIONS

To my colleagues: Kids come first, no matter what. Continuously learn from upsets, missteps, and failure—they are the keys to growth. Do not ignore the signals of error; be intrigued by them, even when it scares you. Relationships matter; work hard to establish and nurture them. Imagine every "big" move or change you make through a teacher's eyes. Remember that you were once in the trenches too. Do the same for parents. Create a team who will speak honestly to you. If you want to build sustainable practices, work to empower those around you. Be reflective. Establish relevant, student-centered, audacious goals with obsessive attention to detail, process, and anticipated outcomes. Be cautious before abandoning goals; instead, be flexible when the process toward achieving goals needs to shift. Never be ashamed or fearful of asking for help; embrace your vulnerabilities, lean on those you respect, and take shamelessly all they can offer. There are stories to be heard and lessons to be learned from all; absorb them and grow your perspective. Be cautious not to make this job your life; it can happen quickly and without warning. Be and stay engaged with the health of you, your family, and friends. When you become consumed or overwhelmed, focus on the people in your life who will love you back. I really learned this the hard way. And through my health ordeal, I am reminded of my own mantra to staff: *"Family and friends first, always."*

Finally, this quote has served me best of all, in work and in life:

> *It is not the critic who counts; not the man who points out how the strong man stumbles, or where the doer of deeds could have done them better. The credit belongs to the man who is actually in the arena, whose face is marred by dust and sweat and blood; who strives valiantly; who errs, who comes short again and again, because there is no effort without error and shortcoming; but who does actually strive to do the deeds; who knows great enthusiasms, the great devotions; who spends himself in a worthy cause; who at the best knows in the end*

the triumph of high achievement, and who at the worst, if he fails, at least fails while daring greatly, so that his place shall never be with those cold and timid souls who neither know victory nor defeat.   - Theodore Roosevelt

Promoting professional collaboration on behalf of increased student learning was the focal point of Beth's leadership. Beth led through her active engagement with her faculty and her self-reflection to coalesce the educators at the Hanscom Primary School. Understanding how teachers viewed leaders, Beth was purposeful in establishing strong, positive and trusting relationships when she returned to Hanscom as its Principal after previously being there as a teacher. Beth wrote, "As a new principal, I had viewed my role as 'selling' my vision to faculty. Over time, I grew to understand that my ability to design a collaborative vision would be the most valuable and sustainable course of action."

In her entry to Hanscom as its leader, Beth established authentic, caring and trusting relationships with faculty and parents. She worked with her faculty to develop a set of school values and rules defining students' behavior expectations. The collaborative work on progressive discipline served as groundwork for the ways teachers planned instruction focused upon improved student learning. The change in the Supervision and Evaluation process state-wide provided an opportunity for Beth to learn alongside her faculty, and she acknowledged the adult learning by saying, "If any part of this lesson fails, we both own it. We will reflect and make improvements for the next lesson together." Additionally, Beth recognized and sought to address the ongoing issue of highly challenging behavior in students: a problem she experienced first-hand and one that weighed heavily on her faculty. Beth offered staff a voluntary summer opportunity to participate in a workshop focused on addressing students' behavior needs. A representative team of teachers chose to engage in the workshop after Beth's first year. She assumed the role of facilitator and co-participant. She invited the team to collaborate on a list of desired outcomes, which resulted in the establishment of the school's Behavioral Emotional Social Support Team (BESST). When school reopened the following fall, the teachers who participated in the summer work presented their plans to the full faculty. The action steps they selected showed that the concerns of all teachers were considered. The process of building a representative team and having teachers communicate with their peers coalesced everyone around the solutions the team developed.

Subsequently Hanscom's BESST model became a district model, used across schools after Beth left Hanscom.

Professional collaboration was at the center of the plan teachers developed to share students across classrooms for reading instruction. In response to the wide range of reading skills in each classroom, teachers worked together to plan groups that included students from multiple classrooms at the same grade level. Bringing students who needed the same instruction together enhanced their learning and enabled teachers to better address student needs.

Moving beyond her building Beth partnered with the middle school principal to introduce a new way of looking at instruction with a priority on how students learn material rather than the content itself. The two leaders established a framework for shifting teachers' perspectives about their practice. Beth states that she learned to "collaboratively reflect, respond, change course, and listen more closely to students and teachers."

5

Mark Nardelli

Horace Mann Elementary School

2010-present

Leadership Story

When I came to Newton's Horace Mann Elementary School, I was following in the footsteps of a popular longtime principal and a one-year interim. Taking this particular position was a bit of a leap professionally; I'd never worked in an elementary school before; my previous teaching experiences and assistant principalship had been at the middle school level. Everything was new to me: the instructional systems, the curriculum, the developmental stages of the students, and the day-to-day operation of the school. Having said that, I wasn't a total stranger to the Horace Mann school community—I had the advantage of having grown up in the neighborhood, and I attended this very same school during the 1970s. Many of the families knew me or my younger brothers, and I had already established some relationships within the community. I think this perhaps helped me to acclimate to this new role.

As a normal part of any new leadership transition within the building, I knew that teachers would begin to gauge what kind of leader I was going to be. I felt that they would wonder about a number of things: Was I going to be visible? Was I going to hold students accountable? What would my stance be on working with parents? In my previous role as a middle school assistant principal, I was lucky enough to work under a principal and administrative team that allowed me to bring my own ideas and structures to the school. I got a lot of firsthand experience with discipline, scheduling, leading faculty professional development, building

Professional Learning Community teams, overseeing crisis management, and much more. My hope was that this experience would give me some practical experience with the challenges that would certainly lay ahead.

I spent the summer before school as well as the majority of the school year talking with school faculty and listening. I set up optional listening conversations for any faculty who wanted to meet with me, and I let them talk about the strengths and areas for growth. Along the way, I began to think about some relatively simple changes I could make as well as some changes that would require more thoughtful collaboration and consensus building. I made it a part of my process to meet with teachers informally as often as possible, and more formally two or three times a year, to check in and to ask questions about how things were going and how I could be helpful. Over the years, these conversations have become a really important way for me to get a sense of staff response to building decisions, to check in about morale, and to gauge interpersonal dynamics.

The Horace Mann community is socioeconomically diverse. Included in the population are families from various income levels and international backgrounds. There are roughly 25 different languages beyond English spoken, with the third-largest population of English language learners (ELLs) in the district of fifteen elementary schools. Shortly after I arrived at Horace Mann, we were designated as a Title I school; we met certain criteria around the percentage of low- income families qualifying us to receive additional Title 1 funding for resources. The population of the school was also in flux. We saw an increase in total population from 370 students to a peak of 430 students over four years. With 19 classrooms and an average class size of 26, we were the most crowded school in the district. In response, the district approved a series of changes to add modular classrooms to the building to increase space and capacity.

September 2010

My tenure at Horace Mann did not start in a way that I might have predicted. On the first day of school, my wife and I didn't quite make it to the hospital, and we delivered our third student in the car on the side of the road in the early hours of the morning. Despite my desire to maintain a low profile at the outset of my tenure, the news of this birth went viral. We had news trucks in front of our school, reporters interviewed families, students (and my mom), and there was a buzz of excitement around the building. I had no plans to take any kind of parental leave as I started this new job, and in the days following Alora's birth, I was back at work. I don't truly know the impact of this start to the school year, but I hoped that this might help establish some basic level of trust that I could manage challenges. And I soon found out that challenges would be waiting for me.

EARLY CHALLENGES: RESPONDING TO BEHAVIORAL /EMOTIONAL NEEDS IN STUDENTS

The culture of the district and this school, in particular, centered around providing an inclusive and welcoming environment for students with a wide range of academic and social needs. Many of the teachers at Horace Mann believed that all students should be included to the greatest extent possible. Despite this belief, one important theme that came up early on in my tenure was the pressure teachers felt to adequately provide for a small subset of students who were presenting with chronic and significant emotional and behavioral needs.

When I came on board, there was one student who was physically destructive and violent for substantial portions of the school day. While teachers did their best to include this student, the faculty felt unable to truly make the student's experience at Horace Mann productive and meaningful. The interim principal before me had rearranged classrooms to make extra space for the student, uprooting other students and teachers. When school started in September, teachers were distraught about the situation and looked to me to develop a path forward. I felt it was important to work directly with this student in hopes of building rapport with this student, and also to demonstrate to the faculty that I was willing to be supportive and to have some credibility when it came time to make some hard decisions.

Despite any direct involvement on my part and additional creative ideas of our faculty, we did not make any meaningful improvement in this student's school experience. By January, we decided that we needed to explore with the family some alternate placement options that would best support this student's short and long term development. Despite the conflicting feelings that members of our faculty felt about the situation, our school was not the right place for this student. It was a difficult decision that took some convincing for some faculty, but I think everybody felt that it was the right thing. For some, it was a welcome relief—even to the inclusion facilitator and school psychologist, who had been the most vocal proponents of inclusion at our school. We all knew that this student would be better off in a place that could more adequately provide the support that the student would need.

This was an important early statement about how far we could go while still being faithful to the idea of inclusion. This case served as a jumping-off point to have more nuanced conversations about our capacity as a school to serve the needs of truly complex students. We had a number of other students who had significant challenges and needed the support of both teachers and special educators, and we needed to think about how we could truly be successful.

During the same year, for one upper grade student, we were able to implement a system of one-on-one check-ins focused on the identified areas for growth. We set up a leadership group for this student and others aimed at providing opportunities to do something positive for the school. This group of students wrote skits aimed at promoting school values; such as kindness and being helpful to others. We filmed the skits and shared the video at our whole school assembly. Our goal was to provide students with a chance to develop a trusting relationship with at least one adult via the one-on-one check-ins as well as to help a given student change the perception that he or she was a troublemaker.

High-needs students created a strain on the classroom teachers who need additional support. Managing and interacting with these students all day long could be emotionally draining. Teachers often felt guilty for not reaching the other students and the distractions that happened did compromise the learning of the other students. When the problems persisted, I felt that as a Principal I had no choice but to say, "Okay, I'll be there. I'll stay in your classroom for the next two hours" or "I'll take the student out of the room." Whether it was me, the psychologist or the behavior interventionist, we all took a role in supporting the classroom teacher. Of course, it was at some cost to my leadership abilities in other areas. I missed grade-level meetings, observations and other responsibilities. However, I felt that addressing the stress on teachers would be more important than pursuing those other tasks.

SCHOOL CULTURE AND VALUES: BUILDING CAPACITY FOR SOCIAL-EMOTIONAL LEARNING

Promoting a positive school culture was my first real initiative at Horace Mann. It started with continuing and adapting a tradition that had been in place when I arrived: monthly all-school assemblies. I was winging it during my first assembly—I had never led one in my life and was terrified that things might devolve into chaos. I decided to focus on a theme for the day; I picked "courage." I stood up in front of 360 students and 60 staff and read a story about courage. We then discussed the different ways you need to have courage and all the different challenges students face. As nerve-racking as it was, I actually really enjoyed being able to get all the students together to talk about something I was passionate about. It was uplifting to have that conversation. Teachers felt empowered to bring these discussions back into their classrooms, and courage became one of our shared beliefs.

In subsequent staff meetings and assemblies, we further examined the values we felt defined us. We spent a great deal of time talking about what was important to us, and "respect," "inclusion," and "making safe choices" became our mantra. We talked about these ideas in our monthly assemblies, and teachers would have more explicit conversations back in the classroom: "What does respect mean on the playground, in the classroom, with adults, with peers?" They came up with examples and brought them to assembly to share with others. Over the next couple of months, we made an effort to recognize these efforts publicly. In essence, it became the first of many schoolwide projects aimed at reinforcing a positive school culture. If a student did something deemed respectful, they could earn a red oval link. At the end of the month we put these links together and draped the hallways with paper chains. Each color represented a value area: blue chains recognized inclusive choices students made, etc. Every student's link represented something positive the students did in one of these value areas.

As we moved forward, each year focused on developing different school values. One year, it was "random acts of kindness." Another year, we created puzzle pieces, where each classroom was responsible for representing a word that Horace Mann stands for—diversity, inclusion, and kindness. One year we "filled buckets." You could fill a bucket by, for example, saying kind things or opening a door for somebody. We tried to sustain the culture by revisiting our values with a slightly different spin each year. These efforts have been an important part of our school culture and have helped to foster a sense of community.

I have grown to learn that the social-emotional aspect of a school culture is the most important variable in determining whether students will be successful in school. I think this is especially true for marginalized populations. I saw this as an area of focus for the school and consequently I spent a good portion of my energy working on initiatives that would support students in this realm.

In my experience, both middle and elementary school populations include a significant number of students who are unable to access the curriculum because they're unavailable for learning. Sometimes the reason for this is really obvious—there are students who are emotionally or behaviorally challenged and perhaps have some kind of diagnosed disability. In other cases, it is less obvious. We had students with attendance issues, anxiety, trauma, and lack of social connections. I came to discover later that other students were less able to learn simply because they felt like an outsider in our school. Regardless of the underlying reasons, our obligation was to provide students with a safe environment.

It appeared that a fair number of students needed sustained, committed opportunities to feel good about themselves, which would in turn translate into more positive attitudes and greater engagement in the classroom. Our internal team came up with a plan to create a behavior intervention position, aimed specifically at working with some of our at-risk population. I engaged in conversations with special education administrators as well as the Superintendent to see if we could come up with a way to fund the position. Eventually, we were able to work out the finances to pilot this program. I agreed to forgo having an assistant principal in exchange for this position. The Behavior Intervention position would be more cost-effective and efficient compared to an assistant principal whose efforts would be diluted across a larger pool of responsibilities. After several years of this program at Horace Mann, the district made the decision to invest in a Behavioral Interventionist in each of the 15 elementary schools.

The Behavior Intervention position grew organically from our original idea. In late October, we began creating a screening tool, which we provided to teachers as a way to identify students who might need support. Using predetermined criteria, we created a list of students at each grade level who are considered at risk and determined varied levels of support that we could put in place. One idea was to create groups that had a theme or a focus, run by the behavior interventionist. For example, we had groups for students who struggled with being kind. We played games, gave them tasks related to kindness, or had them write and act out skits, which we shared at assemblies. For some students who had trouble socializing with peers, we established games-based friendship groups where students had the opportunity to interact with others in a supported environment. We created a fifth-grade leadership team for a particularly challenging group of students. These students were given the opportunity to help monitor the halls in the morning, plan assemblies, work with younger students, or assist with other supportive tasks. We believed that by giving students a chance to receive praise for doing positive things, they would eventually begin to see that they were valued, welcome, and had something to contribute.

Another aspect of the social-emotional arena was work with specific teachers. We noticed that some students experienced greater levels of success in certain classrooms, even when they had struggled in prior years. We began to ask more questions about how our work in social-emotional learning could be focused on supporting teachers. We asked ourselves, "What can teachers do to foster an environment where the students feel safe and welcome?" We provided articles for teachers to read and activities to try, and set up social times with teachers and students to support relationship building.

Thankfully, we weren't alone in our early efforts. The district received a grant to implement a series of programs related to social-emotional learning. A big part of this involved training teachers on a program called Responsive Classroom—an evidence-based approach to content teaching including setting behavior expectations that focuses on engaging academics, positive community, effective management, and developmental awareness. Within a few short years, the majority of our teachers were trained in the Responsive Classroom model. It became the foundation of work that would eventually center around the idea that students must feel connected and loved before they can learn.

THE CHALLENGE OF SCHEDULING STUDENT SUPPORTS

Time is a challenge in every aspect of a school environment. Finding enough time for teachers to collaborate, to plan, to look at student work, to carry out curriculum demands, to consult with many different adults in the building, to train or mentor new teachers are all important and necessary tasks.

Additionally, we were obligated to create a master school schedule that satisfies the requirements laid out by the state. This means finding time for Tier 1 instruction, during which time all students receive high-quality, differentiated, culturally responsive core academic and behavioral instruction through the general education program. Tier 1 time is designed to meet the needs of and ensure positive outcomes for a minimum of 80 percent of all students. In addition to Tier 1 instruction, we had to find additional time in the schedule to implement interventions with a variety of instructional models. The goal of intervention was to meet the needs of the roughly 20 percent of students who needed more time, more practice, or work in smaller groups. Finally, we provided special education services for students who do not respond to intervention and need either specialized accommodations or instruction. The reality is that while we do our best to set priorities and align our time allotments to match our priorities, time continues to be a challenge. We never really have enough time to do the things we want and need to do at the high level of effectiveness we seek

THE NEW INTERVENTION SYSTEM

The first aspect of the new system was building a schedule that allowed for supported literacy intervention in grades K–3. During these designated times, we strategically scheduled our reading faculty to run groups at each grade level. Second, I allocated much of my discretionary aide time toward our literacy program. Five faculty members, all former classroom teachers with some expertise and training in reading instruction, deliver daily small group instruction. We have four groups running based on student level of need. Guided reading, for example, is the least intensive level of support. These groups meet four to five days per week for 20 minutes and are intended for students at or slightly above benchmark. Leveled Literacy Intervention (LLI) is an evidence-based program for our below-benchmark readers. Students in LLI meet in groups of three and receive daily instruction for 30 minutes per session. Third, we have phonics-only groups for students who need to work on encoding and decoding words. These are typically five times per week for 15 minutes per session. Finally, we utilize the Reading Recovery program, which is another evidence-based program for our most struggling early readers. In the Reading Recovery model, first-grade students meet with a teacher daily, one-to-one for 18 to 20 weeks using a highly structured lesson format. There are indicators that the school is making progress with these interventions in place. Last year, for example, all 12 of the first-graders receiving LLI showed at least three levels of growth on their Benchmark Literacy Assessment in just two months' time. Over the same time period, three students showed four levels of growth, and one showed five. In addition, we did not refer any students for special education evaluation during those months.

POSITIVE IMPACT ON SPECIAL EDUCATION REFERRALS

Prior to our current intervention system, special education was the only available service for struggling learners. A student who needed extra reading support would need to qualify for special education in order to receive that additional instruction. The problem with that model was that it essentially waited for kids to fail before they could access support. When students get far enough behind, we can evaluate them, show that they had a diagnosed disability, needed the specialized assistance, and then developed the IEP (Individualized Educational Program) with recommended services. Barriers existed to the implementation of special education services: special educators must attend team meetings and complete testing, provide compensatory services for any that were missed due to fulfilling those responsibilities, consult with teachers, and respond to students when they are having behavioral challenges. Students rarely made up lost ground when they received an Individual Educational Program (IEP). Shifting to a regular education model of intervention with Reading Recovery and LLI there were almost zero interruptions to services and the students got what they needed from the outset, rather than falling behind.

Due to the intervention model we put in place, we've had a significant drop in special education referrals. During the 2017–2018 school year, we didn't evaluate a single first-grader for learning concerns compared to the average three to five first-grade referrals. Over the past three years, we have decreased our IEP caseload from 100 to 40 students. The vast majority of evaluations have been done based on parent requests. This isn't a commentary on parents; they are simply advocating for their students. However, the vast majority of parent requests have not resulted in the student qualifying for special education. We strongly believe in our intervention system, which in many ways is better than what we can offer in special education. Our interventions are more consistent, we have a highly trained faculty, and we can offer students more time in small groups.

Over the years, I have come to believe that the special education system is in need of rethinking. The program at Horace Mann is no exception. A typical special education model has a couple of faculty who are tasked with providing academic and social/behavioral services to our most vulnerable students. Special education teachers often have a large caseload, work with multiple general education teachers, and are required to have knowledge of the K–5 curriculum. Special educators are supposed to serve all the identified students, but they are constantly interrupted for meetings, student testing, behaviors, and more. For teachers, these services get interrupted leaving students at a disadvantage in the classroom. Continuity of service is interrupted for the students, who can least afford to miss these opportunities for small group and one-on-one instruction.

In addition to instituting a more robust intervention program in our early grades, we modified the grade 4 and 5 model by creating co-taught classrooms. Co-taught classrooms have three adults in the room full-time—a classroom teacher, a special educator, and a graduate intern. The teams have been a great success for a number of reasons: there are fewer interruptions, the teachers need to know a much narrower range of curriculum, and services are delivered right in the classroom. Over the years, students have demonstrated solid progress in this model.

Positive Impact on Student Social-Emotional Health

We have seen positive results in the social-emotional realm as well. We haven't referred a student for evaluation for social-emotional or behavioral concerns for about six years. In comparison to other schools in the district, we are a true anomaly. Our school has rarely needed the support of a citywide behavior intervention program. Schools call this team to consult with building-based behavior specialists for students who are really struggling. The district team comes in to do observations, create and implement intervention plans, and provide staffing support. Over the last six years, we have called the team twice to consult about students. This incidence is much lower than most of the other district schools, who utilize the team multiple times each year.

Our school data supports our positive results, illustrated well by one student's journey. One young student was struggling significantly. They exhibited task avoidance: refusal to write, read, or do math. They shut down frequently, were defiant and disrespectful, and periodically showed explosive and destructive behavior. A team of adults consulted on a regular basis to think about the underlying reasons for the behavior and to come up with interventions to address it. We created behavior plans, implemented non-contingent breaks, came up with incentives, modified work demands, set up snack groups, and more. Even with all the modifications, we struggled throughout the entire year. There were some faculty members who felt that we should just do an evaluation or advocate for mental health support, as if these steps would offer some quick fix. I pushed our faculty to avoid this, and in the following academic year, we added additional academic support with teachers who could establish a strong connection with the student. By midyear the student began to read, accept constructive feedback, and engage in far fewer negative behaviors. It wasn't perfect by any means, but the interventions were clearly working. By the fall of the third year, this student had become a whole new person. The student engaged in classroom work, talking about things that bothered them, persevered through difficult academic tasks, and began connecting with more peers. Although they still had their moments, overall we were able to address the student's feelings of mistrust, being unwelcome, and being an inadequate learner. The student didn't need a special education evaluation, but rather love, warmth, and scaffolded support that would help highlight small successes at school.

FOSTERING TEACHER ENGAGEMENT AND LEADERSHIP

It is important to point out that our programs and decision-making were not all coming from me. I'm not an expert, and I've had great people on my team who really know what they are talking about. It has always been important to me that I listen to teachers' perspectives and involve them in many of the decisions that our school needs to make.

At one point, my first-grade team came to me for support around a problem they were having with progress monitoring. This team had consistently been strong and collaborative, and prior to my arrival, they had spearheaded an intervention that I wanted to promote and expand. Collaboration with a capital "C" was something I emphasized from the get-go. The first-grade team had developed benchmarks and regular periodic assessments to identify at-risk students, but they needed some staffing help to carry out the plan. They developed a proposal showing how they could implement their plan. My task was to find time in the schedule and identify faculty to carry out certain elements of the plan. Together, we were able to bring a good idea to fruition.

In another example, when I was asked for input from the city about some decisions related to our facility and use of space, I formed a team that was composed of teachers who were able to offer invaluable input into our programming decisions. This included placement of classrooms, lockers, safe spaces, etc. Without teacher input, I would have made decisions that would have made things harder for teachers and students in their daily work.

As we began our equity work, I relied heavily on several faculty members who had a strong background in working with adults on issues related to gender identity and race. They formed the foundation of a group that took on the responsibility for planning professional development opportunities for our faculty. Time and time again, I have come to appreciate the essential role that teachers play in making decisions for the school, and it has become an integral part of my leadership approach.

Teachers are at the center of the school and I trust them to make important decisions every day. Not blind trust, but rather trust that's supported by thoughtful reasoning. The school was fortunate to have veteran teachers who were true experts. Teachers know their students; they know what works or doesn't work and need to have some latitude in making decisions. When a new approach to a curricular area is introduced, I start by trusting their judgment and instincts and work to encourage consideration of the new programs to add to their already extensive teaching repertoire.

Collaboration is an essential part of our school culture. Teachers who talk, learn, and reflect together often make better decisions than those who simply make them on their own. For example, one source of frustration for our teachers was around the city's data collection system. The system asked teachers to regularly fill in spreadsheets of information without allowing them to manipulate or access the data. If they wanted a specific breakdown of the information, they would have to request it from the data office and wait two weeks to get it.

As a school, we muddled through the use of this data system before deciding we needed to improve it. As a group, we sat down and talked about software we could use. It wasn't rocket science—just a Google spreadsheet on a shared platform that could be used in real time. It quickly became a living, breathing document that teachers could actually use to make instructional decisions. Initially, we got pushback from the district literacy coordinator, who wanted to continue using the old system. However, we were able to quickly demonstrate the simplicity and flexibility of the new system, and the city soon adopted a model based on our original Google spreadsheet.

The lesson here is that teachers need to be heard and their input and classroom decision-making needs to be honored. Teachers are professional, they are smart, and they can do really good work when they are treated with respect and their judgment is sought after and valued. A huge part of my job is making sure that teachers feel supported. I look out for them and provide opportunities for them to do what they are supposed to be doing—teaching the students.

Building a Culturally Responsive School

Over the first few years, I really felt that we were in a good place in terms of how we treated each other. I naively thought that we had built a culture of respect in open mindedness and acceptance, and one that was shielded from the hate and intolerance in the world. However a series of things happened to change my perspective: some second-graders using the n-word on the playground; a student telling me in my office that there were no Asian lead characters in the books he was reading; a fourth-grader making negative comments about "strange food" that another student had brought for lunch that day.

The particular event that crystallized the fact that we still had a lot of work to do occurred when, on the first day back from summer vacation, a student shared with their class, "I'm transgender. Actually, I think I'm gender-fluid. Sometimes, I would like to come to school dressed as a boy and sometimes dressed as a girl." This announcement wasn't terribly surprising; there had been signs that this student was questioning their gender identity. We saw emotional ups and downs, behaviors with peers that were disconcerting and atypical. Looking back, this student was clearly trying to communicate some greater distress. It awakened in me the realization that others may be going through similar struggles. It took the courage of one student to help me understand that our school and our broader society could potentially be unwelcoming and possibly threatening.

I began to seriously consider other scenarios: perhaps students were hesitant to share something about their religion or that their parents were here illegally. Perhaps students were experiencing negative interactions with their peers about the color of their skin, or the fact that they had two moms at home. Perhaps some of this came out in the form of negative behaviors that were really attempts at communicating some underlying level of discomfort or some reluctance to share a part of their identity.

Our school really needed to have a mission: to create an environment that would be welcoming to all. For one student it meant working with their family, our staff, and outside professionals to figure out what we needed to do or learn to help this student feel safe and supported. We held workshops around LGBTQ issues for our faculty. We wrote letters to the community, and we were vigilant in our daily support of this student's journey. By the following year, the student felt comfortable enough to live their preferred identity. After this experience I began to look at our students with a more thoughtful eye.

What had previously seemed like little examples of bias became more obvious to me because I was really paying attention. I did some reading. A couple of books in particular changed my view of the world. *The New Jim Crow* and *The Divide* were really eye-opening and took away any thoughts I had about racism being a thing of the past. I went from a place of relative privilege and naiveté about other people's experiences to saying, "Wait a minute. I've got a whole population of students who might not feel as safe here as I initially thought."

For the past number of years, we've been extremely committed to becoming more culturally responsive. All of our professional development has been created with this lens in mind. One fifth-grade teacher at our school is a former E.M.I. (Empowering Multicultural Initiatives) trainer and has a lot of experience working with teachers around issues related to race. E.M.I. is "a coordinated effort to improve the academic achievement of students of color while nurturing the growth and development of all students, and to promote systemic anti-racist practices and culturally relevant teaching through faculty training and leadership development." Early on, this teacher and I developed a series of activities centered on making school a safe place regardless of your family structure, gender identity, socioeconomic status, race, or religion. We then expanded to include several other faculty members. We now meet at least once a month to plan additional pieces of this work, which encompasses several professional learning strands.

One strand is whole staff learning. In the current political climate, people seem unwilling to hear someone else's perspective, walk in their shoes, or believe that their experience could be different. Perspective is a big part of this work and raising awareness through the use of storytelling has been a central approach to our thinking. As such, we designed and taught activities that had a storytelling component. We had high school students speak to our whole staff about what it was like to go through the Newton public schools as a student of color: "I just wish somebody pronounced my name the right way"; "I just wish somebody had pushed me a little harder instead of accepting a story that could clearly be better"; " I just wish I had read a story that had an Asian protagonist in it before my junior year in high school." Rather than simply highlight the statistics and discuss the relevance of the data, we felt that personal stories were the most powerful way to convey the need for change. When a story strikes a chord with teachers, they are much more likely to act in response.

One strand focused on creating a mini-curriculum aimed at having explicit conversations about identity, privilege, and diversity. We created a series of lessons on anti-bias and anti-prejudice to be completed with students. We had a group pull those lessons together and publish the document to share with the rest of the faculty (and eventually with the district). At that time, there was no place in the curriculum where this material was taught explicitly. So the whole faculty worked to create lessons that we thought should be taught at each grade level. We are continuously updating them: Which topics were really strong? What could be included or omitted? The expectation was that teachers dedicate three lessons a year in each grade to one of the identified topics.

In second grade, for example, teachers taught a lesson early in the year called "Who is my family?" where they talk about different kinds of family and read different stories. This idea is not new, nor is it profound, but we included the lesson in the materials because we had a student who had been apprehensive about being "person of the week." They didn't want to participate because they had two moms at home and thought they would be teased for their family structure. The aim of this lesson was to create a classroom culture that would send the message that all kinds of families are welcome at Horace Mann. Ultimately, we want each student to be able to feel comfortable with who they are.

Another strand we felt was important was to provide choice for teachers. Just as we do with students, teachers need to have some say in what they are learning to stay invested. We brainstormed a list of things that we could do to make our school more culturally responsive, and teachers could choose what they wanted to work on that would impact their practice and the experience of students.

Teachers worked in groups on a variety of topics; some chose to focus on having more diverse texts in classrooms, others worked on broadening perspectives in history, while others focused on the physical appearance of the school. In this last group, teachers designed a mural with students from all different backgrounds. We intentionally included a scene where students were wearing hijabs. The next day, we had four girls come to school wearing their own hijab for the first time. There's no question that what we were doing was important.

We included a strand focused on parent outreach. We felt that it was important to provide an opportunity for parents to understand our mission as a school, and to engage in their own learning around issues related to equity. To this end, we tried to implement several initiatives to connect our work to families. Early on in the year, my back-to-school night speech highlighted our equity work. We also held a number of workshops for parents. For example, with fifth-grade students and parents, we hold an annual evening screening of a video called Not in Our Town. It's about a white nationalist group committing hate crimes in Billings, Montana, primarily aimed at a Jewish family. We then talk about how we can actively combat racism and hatred. We've done workshops on white privilege, diverse literature, and growth mindset, among other topics. In addition, we've worked with our parent group to create a more welcoming atmosphere for families. We moved International Night to the fall, expanded our Book Fair selection to offer more diverse texts, created support systems for families in the METCO Program (Inner-city students enroll in school in neighboring suburban communities) to attend evening events, and offered student care for all families so parents and caregivers can attend school events. Finally, we've created a parent-led group to run evening conversations about race based on videos we've watched or books we've read.

We've got a long way to go with regard to the cultural responsiveness piece, but we are doing things that we hope connect the dots for students. We've got to move toward more instruction and how instruction could look different depending on culture. That's the learning we're doing right now.

As a white person in a white culture, I spent a lot of my life being oblivious to the experiences of others, and I think it's my responsibility to help our faculty realize that they also play a primary role in that. Together, we have to be willing to acknowledge our own identity, our own sense of what we know or don't know about our community, and then try to connect to the things that we haven't ever been asked to do because we're in the dominant cultures.

An important part of this initiative is how we measure progress. We're just in the beginning stages of putting together all of the different variables that we think might have something to do with the work, whether it's disciplinary, special education or behavior team referrals, Massachusetts state test scores, feedback from parents after a workshop or any initiative. I'm not sure how we're going to definitively say, "This outcome is a direct result of this effort or activity." My ultimate hope would be that we see gains in academics that show a decrease in the gap between the majority population and the marginalized groups. The hope is that helping students succeed here will help them have a better shot at achieving their goals outside of the classroom. That's the challenge now. How do we measure some of what we're doing so that over time we have some data from year to year that identifies successes and highlights areas for continued growth.

I've always valued social and racial justice and have wanted to advocate for the underprivileged, but I definitely had a naive view of what the world really is like now. I can no longer deny there's a tangible distance in experience for students depending on where they come from and what they look like. I didn't see the systems that have entrenched these racist and discriminatory beliefs and experiences. I had no idea when I was growing up, that Newton itself was an area where some people were pretty deliberate about making sure that mostly white folks ended up here.

It's clear where we want to go. It's just a matter of how we're going to get as many people as possible there with us. There is no "there" really—no end point. It's a journey and we'll all just improve along the way; some more quickly than others.

I don't want to be viewed as a savior or a rescuer. This isn't about some privileged white guy swooping in with a cape. I don't want that to be the perception. So that's the only problem I have when I think about this work.

The superintendent and the district have increasingly seen the importance of equity as a central focus of our work. Our meetings, our small group work, our visits to schools, our professional development, are all focused on equity. There are family conferences with workshops on race, and we are increasing efforts to hire more diverse teachers and administrators. It feels good to be supported in this work rather than being on an island by myself.

LEADING DURING COVID-19

March 13, 2020 - We received word on this date that schools would be shut down temporarily in response to the emerging concerns around the spread of Covid-19 virus. The next several months were among the most stressful for educators and administrators due to the immediate requirement that we pivot to an entirely new method of teaching students. In a very short time, we were faced with learning new technologies, including Zoom/Google Meet, and a variety of online learning platforms. The district also had huge challenges supporting efforts to educate students in their homes. This included acquiring technology (laptops, hotspots, etc), as well as classroom materials like math books, sets of letter tiles, books, and a hundred other items.

This was all done under significant frustration and scrutiny from a parent population who immediately put pressure on teachers and administrators to implement a viable online instructional model. Some teachers picked up the technology and the format more quickly than others. There were also great differences between 4th and 5th graders and their ability to manage technology as well as their attention span. In contrast, younger students needed a lot of adult support to get online at home, putting tremendous stress on parents and caregivers to juggle both work and online school. These variables created increased pressure from parents who were comparing experiences across classrooms and grade levels, and demanding that schools adjust very quickly to a whole new way of doing business. The spring of 2020 was very stressful for all involved.

May 2020 - The death of George Floyd also had a significant impact on our school and on our teaching faculty, as was true all across the country. At Horace Mann, George Floyd's death served as an important moment for our white teachers, in particular. As an extension of the work we had been doing as a faculty to create a more culturally responsive school, our teachers felt that they needed more time to talk about concepts related to race and its connection to racial identity. One of our teacher leaders and I crafted a plan to form a voluntary group that would meet weekly after school hours to watch videos, read articles, and have discussions about race. I participated in the first two sessions, but as a group, we decided that my presence as an administrator might inhibit staff's willingness to truly be open about their experiences. So, the group formed a small planning team, and they carried on with the work without my participation. This work continued weekly throughout the spring and summer months, with teachers meeting weekly via Zoom. It is hard to quantify the outcomes of this work, but anecdotally, I can say that there has been a shift on the part of some of our faculty to see our work in a different light. For example, I had a kindergarten teacher offer to take on a new student of color coming to our school who had significant struggles at his former school. We ignored typical variables like class size in favor of other ideas that we felt would help the student make an easier transition and a greater chance of success in school. Other examples include greater reflection on the part of teachers in a variety of settings: pre-referral meetings, discussions about behavior of a student, etc. Teachers are open to the idea that the experiences of students of color may need a different lens, particularly from the perspective of a white teacher.

June-August 2020 - Teachers got a little bit of a break during the summer of 2020, but school administrators worked throughout the summer to figure out how we could improve on the learning model of the previous spring. We were also at the mercy of state and to a lesser extent, federal decision making bodies who were laying out guidelines and expectations for the various school models that could be run.

Our district surveyed parents multiple times to determine their level of comfort in sending their students to school. The district also had to keep a pulse on the teachers' unions who would also determine whether teachers would feel safe enough to return to the classroom.

Model: After many lengthy days of discussions and data collection, the district made the decision to create a hybrid in-person model as well as an entirely remote model for learning in the 2020-2021 school year. The hybrid model consisted of students coming to school two days per week, and doing three days of remote learning. This also meant that teachers would have to plan for both in-person instruction as well as create remote learning assignments. For the remote learning model, teachers either volunteered or were assigned to teach a class entirely online.

As administrators, we were tasked with redoing class placement, creating both new in-person and entirely remote classes. We also planned for a way to accommodate high needs students so they could attend school in-person more than twice a week. We also planned for students of educators to attend school five days per week. A smaller group (myself included) created the teaching sections for the remote learning program, which included classes containing students from multiple schools across the district. The logistics around all of this was intense for school administrators.

Building Preparations - A related aspect of this work included creating conditions in the building to allow for physical distancing. We had to identify and remove furniture and set up classrooms with desks 6 feet apart. We moved cafeteria tables, created eating spaces in the gym, added ventilation, etc. Again, school administrators were a focal point of implementation and communication.

School Schedule - In addition to the class placement and building preparations, we also had to create all new schedules to reflect the hybrid learning structure. We created an in-school schedule, as well as remote schedules that contained specials (art, music, library, and pe), which were entirely online.

Throughout the course of the year, with changing guidelines from the state, we adjusted our schedules several times. Families were given the option to change learning models at various stages, and learning models changed. In April, the most significant of the changes was implemented: students returned to school full time. This again required a shift to an all new schedule, modifications to classroom placements, etc.

Instruction - During the hybrid stages of the academic model, Covid prevented small group work and fewer opportunities to work with students in person on targeted instructional goals. While teachers did have smaller classes (8-10 students) two days per week, they were unable to do small reading groups due to health and safety requirements. We did implement literacy intervention groups with our intervention faculty, but instead of meeting 5 times per week, students were typically seen only 3 times per week (with one of those sessions happening on Zoom). Despite this, we felt that the students got a chance to work on basic reading skills and many of the students made progress. At the end of the year, all but one of our students in Kindergarten had met the end of year reading benchmark.

Tragedy - Adding to the significant stress of the 2020-21 school year, we also faced the loss of one our beloved 5th grade teachers, who endured a short but intense battle with cancer. The loss was really hard on all of us and added substantially to the challenges of an already difficult year.

2021-22 School Year - Moving into the fall of 2021, with the prevalence of the vaccine, administrators and teachers expected to have an easier year than the previous one. However, that turned out not to be the case at all.

One concern was the fact that we welcomed a substantial number of students back to our school (almost 25% of our pre-Covid population) back to the school building after an 18 month absence. Some of the students had been in a private setting, some were in the distance learning academy, and a small number were homeschooled.

Academically, the impact was apparent early in the fall. Our Kindergarten cohort, now in first grade, saw a 25% influx of students compared to when we had left school in June. While many of our K students were at benchmark in June, a substantial number of the students who had not been with us were significantly below the expected grade level benchmark. This is a trend we also saw in grades 2 and 3, in particular.

This fall, the district also implemented a series of new assessments, partially to comply with state guidelines around dyslexia screening. The new assessments are very different from our previous assessments, making it difficult to use instructional data and to interpret growth data. Anecdotally, we know that overall, our students are performing at lower levels than we would have expected at each grade level, but because the assessments are so different, we are still adapting to what the data is telling us. One other data point is also important to note: we have had a significant uptick in the number of referrals for special education, both from concerned teachers, as well as from families. We are not sure if the increase is due to expectations that are being measured at pre-pandemic levels of achievement, or if students are more clearly showing signs of a potential disability, perhaps induced by the pandemic and the tumultuous schooling experiences of the past two years.

In the social-emotional realm, the vast majority of our students K-5 were behind where we expected them to be. Kindergarten teachers expressed concerns that students were developmentally more like preschoolers. They have described students as having more difficulty internalizing classroom routines, managing conflicts (sharing materials, taking turns, etc.), gauging the size of a problem, managing reactions to events, and dealing with stress, to name a few. Teachers have had to re-teach routines and be explicit about expected behaviors. In response, I have been intentional about providing resources to teachers to address the deficits we are seeing across the school. Each month, I have shared lessons, activities, read-alouds, and discussions from the citywide CARES curriculum, with the expectations that teachers would be spending time on these lessons each week.

Stress on Faculty - In addition, many teachers have displayed signs of their own struggles with challenges taking place outside of school. Juggling family members with Covid, daycare closings, significant family trauma and illness, and many other issues have added significant stress and taken a toll on the mental health of staff. This has been evident in a variety of ways: we've had faculty taking time off to take care of family members, taking days off for mental health, taking requests to take part time leaves of absence, processing emotions and struggles with teachers, etc. It isn't clear how much the stress on teachers might be impacting students, but there is a noticeable difference in the building with regard to outward expressions of joy and laughter. What was once plentiful, is now more rare.

Traditions - Many things changed over the course of the pandemic with regard to school culture.

Faculty - Early on, teachers spent more time planning together to share the workload, particularly with regard to the remote lessons they were tasked with planning each week. Over time, though, due to social distancing requirements and the sheer time demands of the job, teachers increasingly became isolated. Faculty couldn't eat lunch together, we had no social gatherings, faculty meetings were on Zoom, etc. Grade level teams and PLC groups met less frequently, if at all, and we've found that this isolation has endured and become a new habit that will be hard to break.

Students and Families - We have also become more fractured as a student community. Where we once held monthly all school assemblies, we now have occasional videos that teachers show in class. The goal of the assemblies is to come together to share stories, reinforce values, kickoff schoolwide projects, celebrate, and have fun. Not having assemblies has limited our ability to feel that we are part of a bigger community.

We also had to give up many of the things that brought our community together - Science Night, Food and Culture Night, Talent Show, and Fitness for Life are all in-person events that had to either be canceled or turned into a virtual event. These are all significant losses in our efforts to be inclusive, welcoming and connected as a community. It also takes away from our ability to celebrate our diversity.

February 2022 - In recent weeks, we have begun to pull back on the stringent guidelines around health and safety. We've pulled back on weekly Covid testing, and will soon be relaxing mask guidelines. It is hard to say at this point what the implications of this are, but we are looking forward to planning some of our more normal events for the spring in the hopes of bringing the community back together.

Although he had never led an all-school assembly for elementary students and staff before, at the first monthly all-school assembly of his tenure at Horace Mann Mark proposed the value "courage," for discussion by faculty and students. His approach to identifying core values, including students and staff in the conversation, was indicative of Mark's leadership style. He modeled coalescing a school community through open, honest dialogue. Subsequently the Horace Mann School would collectively determine that "courage" and other positive values would be included in the Core Purposes that defined the school's educational vision. Mark's own courage in sharing one of his core beliefs embodied his desire to engage everyone in the process of articulating the school's mission. Faculty and students would be party to setting the future course of the school.

Mark acknowledged his predisposition to observing the effects of social-emotional phenomena. He recognized the need for social emotional learning to take center stage and serve as a foundation for improved student learning. As a result of his observations when he entered the school, Mark was able to highlight for the faculty how this phenomenon was inhibiting student learning; students were not available for learning in the classroom. The etiology ranged from the severity of diagnosed disabilities to students feeling like "outsiders" in their school. Led by Mark, faculty implemented change efforts for at-risk students with behavior issues. He provided opportunities to identify and then elevate at-risk students using positive experiences to improve their self-concept and decrease disruptive behaviors. With Mark's guidance, the faculty started viewing this cohort of students differently. Shifting from a negative view, the teachers worked collaboratively to develop a set of positive interactions between students and their peers as well as with their teachers. The faculty grouped at-risk students into teams with similar learning challenges. The teams of students were guided by adults in the school as they explored how they might give value to others. In addition to lifting up others, those at-risk students had the potential for increased self-esteem. Mark noted a specific example stating, "A particularly challenging group of students were given the opportunity to help monitor the halls in the morning, plan school assemblies, work with younger students and assist with other supportive tasks." The possibility of receiving praise for doing positive things was posited as a means of communicating to the students to know they were valued, welcomed and had something to contribute to the entire community. A second example was the hallway displays of core value chains; recognizing exemplary individual actions in a visual manner that the entire school participated in and celebrated. These activities were in keeping with Mark's strategy to coalesce the school using positive activities as key elements in a reconfigured culture.

Connecting social emotional well being with academic success was a clear goal for Mark. With district support, he had faculty trained in the Responsive Classroom model. Responsive Classroom combines setting guidelines for academic success for every member with student and teacher involvement in building the behavior expectations that guide the classroom community.

Mark translated the issues he observed from students with significant behavior needs into a school wide structure for intervening to support students before issues arose. He successfully challenged Horace Mann faculty teams to demonstrate how the services could be improved by assuming the responsibility for delivering the service rather than having the district personnel intervene. Mark's leadership enabled staff to pro-actively respond to student needs and dramatically reduce the number of students requiring special education services. Horace Mann faculty developed a simple, flexible system that enabled teachers to manipulate the data in support of teaching and learning. Joining with the faculty, Mark was instrumental in significantly improving the quality and timeliness of services provided to students with identified special needs. By responding to teacher teams and their observations of students, Mark reconfigured the schedule to provide additional faculty for literacy intervention in primary grade classrooms and co-teaching models in upper grades. The message he sent to the faculty affirmed their ability to support their students regardless of need: he acted by putting the resources where they were needed. As a result, Horace Mann teachers implemented inspiring practices that others in the District sought to emulate.

Mark's sensitivity to social/emotional health in the school led him to re-evaluate his perspective regarding how Horace Mann faculty responded to the diverse student population in the building. He utilized the specific instances with students in the school to build urgency among faculty, and partnered with the district-wide focus on the topic of cultural responsiveness. The faculty worked together to consider the diversity of their community and bring increased awareness to the students and their families. Recognizing the strength and personal connections of individual stories, Mark invited High School students to speak, as well as sharing situations involving Horace Mann students. Listening to their personal experiences had a powerful impact on the students and faculty, moving them forward in their learning about culturally responsive teaching. The Horace Mann community came together to learn and deepen their understanding of the impact of privilege and how they could respond with active anti-racist words and deeds.

His guidance translated into faculty engagement and collective action coalescing the school with a goal of heightened student efficacy and emotional well-being, expanded family engagement in the work of the school and most importantly, improved student learning.

6

Manuel J. Fernandez

Cambridge Street Upper School

March-June 2021

Leadership Story

AFTER HIGH SCHOOL, my goal in life was to be the manager of the Bradlees's department store in the Westgate Mall. I pursued this dream, until it hit me—I just wasn't into it. I found myself making a series of irresponsible decisions, ultimately ending up jobless.

An older gentleman, who I had known since my studenthood, saw me hanging out at a park day after day.

"What are you doing?" he asked me.

I replied honestly: "Nothing"

He challenged me: "We used to talk about you becoming a lawyer. I guess my expectations for you were too high."

He got me involved in an anti-poverty agency. I started having fun doing that; we had after school tutoring for kids, camping trips, concerts, carnivals, and all kinds of things of that sort.

That same gentleman approached me one morning and said, "Look, they have this program at Southeastern Massachusetts University, where guys like you, who weren't necessarily prepared for college, can spend five years getting a four-year degree." I applied and was accepted. I visited him in hospice this last summer to tell him how impactful he had been in my life.

He was only the second adult to suggest to me that I should go to college, the first being a white male teacher in my senior year who helped me enroll in community college. I quit after the first semester because

I had not been prepared to go to college and had never taken a college prep course. My late mentor was a Black man who himself had enrolled in college many years after high school. He helped me understand that my reticence to go to college was because of an internalized belief that as Black men, we were not capable of succeeding in college. He sent the message, "I did, and so can you."

Next thing I knew, I was on campus. And by mid-October, I was the vice president of the Black Student Union and a senator in the student government. I was very engaged in politics in school. People saw in me a leadership ability that I didn't necessarily see in myself. I was shy and insecure, but when I got on a roll, the passion would come flooding out.

By the point of graduation, I was the student body president. It still shocks the hell out of me because there were 5,000 students, only 300 of them Black, and there I was, the president of the entire student body. It was my first leadership experience that extended beyond the Black community. My plan after graduation was to become a social worker and save the world. During my junior year, I began tutoring students in the Upward Bound program. Whereas working as a social work intern I felt my work was reactive, as a tutor I felt proactive. I could see my work personified through my students' success in class and on assessments.

I started my public school career as a middle school METCO counselor in a small, wealthy, predominantly white town located about 30 minutes outside of Boston, Massachusetts. (METCO stands for Metropolitan Council for Educational Opportunity, a program intended to expand educational opportunities, increase diversity, and reduce racial isolation by permitting students in Boston to attend public schools in other participating communities). The majority of students I worked with were Black and Latino.

In my sixth year, the METCO director went on leave, and I took over the position. I wasn't very good at it—I didn't have any role models, and I left the position after one year. After spending two years away, I was asked to return to the district as the METCO director. I spent 12 years in that role. I learned my leadership skills through my involvement in the METCO Directors Association, and I eventually became its president.

I'm blessed with the gift of being a strong communicator. People would say, "He's such a good speaker; he should be our president!"

Joining with seven other METCO directors and our district superintendents, we founded a highly successful nonprofit organization, Eastern Massachusetts Initiative (EMI), which trained thousands of Eastern Massachusetts public school teachers and administrators in anti-racism and diversity. I was proud to be a part of the beginnings. Its mission mirrored my own values, but also shaped the leadership vision that motivates me to this day. I became the first executive director of EMI.

After I had been at METCO in my two stints for 18 years, I needed to get out. One reason was that in a white upper-class community, my expectations for Black and Latino students were different from a lot of other people's. If a METCO student wanted to play football or basketball or some other sport but got a grade below a C, I would tell their parents that they shouldn't be allowed to play. Generally, I was overruled or, I should say, outmaneuvered by coaches, administrators, and the district, who were basically saying, "But Massachusetts guidelines state that kids can get all Ds and still be eligible to play." Coaches would go directly to the superintendent and parents and say my expectations were unfair; and in one case, it was suggested it was discriminatory to hold METCO students to a different standard. For me, it was a losing battle.

The other reason was that METCO was not as enduring as it had once been. Some residents moving into the METCO communities were questioning the program. There was pushback saying it wasn't necessary. After a while, it seemed to me the fight was essential, but my currency as one of the warriors was not effective. It was a constant cycle. Each year, I would try to figure out how to get those 120 kids of color to succeed in a population of 2,000 white students. I started feeling, looking, and acting like the angry Black man. So I started looking for a new job.

First Principalship: Xonward Charter School

Someone from Xonward Charter School came to me and said, "We're looking for a principal." I didn't have a license, but they said because it was a charter school, a license wouldn't be necessary. They mentioned that people were interested in me because they found my leadership abilities effective. That August, I became the principal. The school defined itself as being teacher-driven, but most of the teachers were fresh out of college and didn't have the experience in diverse school communities to effectively drive its mission. Also, Xonward was conceived as a place that would rival Boston Latin, one of the most—if not the most—prestigious exam schools in Boston, but with more diversity. It seemed clear to me that it wasn't going to be like that. Unlike Latin, where you have to take an exam to gain acceptance, the youngsters at Xonward were picked through a random lottery system. Their skill sets ranged significantly, the student population was predominantly of color and the school wasn't prepared to handle that.

I hired more people of color, as there weren't many when I started. The school didn't recognize the need to have more discussions about race and culture, and my decisions could be overturned by teachers at a Friday meeting, even if I had previously sent out communications about the decision with my name on it. That got frustrating.

I knew I had made a mistake by November 1st but kept it to myself. By February, I learned that the school agreed with me. Just before February vacation, a student came to me and asked, "Mr. Fernandez, are you leaving?"

I was confused and asked him what he meant. He said, "Oh I just walked past the teachers' room and I heard them talking about when you were going to leave."

It turned out that a group of teachers had gathered as a cabal to develop a presentation for the board about why I should be let go. I was bitter that they had gone behind my back like that. There was nothing transparent about the place whatsoever.

The white chairman of the board and the only Black board member sat me down. They said bluntly, "You don't have the support of a lot of the faculty, and we're not going to renew your contract next year." When I left at the end of the year, there was no applause, nobody saying goodbye or wishing me well. A few had said things to me personally, but there was no party. I was just out the back door.

My biggest win was that I knew I didn't have the right skill set to be a principal of a predominantly white faculty that didn't see that race and culture matter in schools. I didn't know how to respond to the push back challenging discussions about race and the opportunity gap. What made it worse was that my ego was too fragile, particularly when I encountered things I didn't know. Unlike new principals today, I didn't have a mentor to guide me and support me.

Every time someone would question my leadership or a decision or disagree with the position or the direction that the school was going, I took it personally. It ate me up and made me feel insecure. I couldn't be nimble. I couldn't move from here to there, I just fell deeper and deeper into the hole. I had taken the job to get away from METCO, but I had leaped before I looked. Another takeaway was that, because of the emotional toll, I didn't want to be a high school administrator again. Middle school kids' missteps can break your heart from time to time, but when a high school kid missteps, it not only breaks your heart, it can have devastating effects for them. Decisions that they make in high school either end up on a transcript or lead to them not having one at all.

PRINCIPAL FELLOWS PROGRAM: BOSTON PUBLIC SCHOOLS

After Xonward, my work did not sustain me. I was doing diversity consulting for charter schools and traveling around the country doing corporate diversity work for a private consulting firm. It was easy, high-paid work, but it was soulless. What kept nagging me was, nothing stuck. I wasn't building capacity. 9/11 determined the end of that work. Many of my clients had been in New York and ceased operations and so my corporate consulting career was suspended.

When I first applied to the Principal Fellows Program within the Boston Public Schools, I figured I had a snowball's chance in Hell of being accepted. I was up against 50 other applicants. I was older—in my 40s. I'd been knocked down a couple of times and taken some hits to my self-confidence. As part of the application process, they ran us through a series of exercises, simulating what principals do. When they scored me, they said, "You were pretty high on everything except 'observation and evaluation.'" This didn't come as a surprise. I'd never been a licensed teacher, and in my earlier positions, evaluation wasn't a priority.

The Fellows program taught me that I do well working with others, having people pick my brain, and having the opportunity to pick theirs. It allows us to push each other. That's what the Fellows cohort was all about. My mentor was one of the district's star principals. She taught me a lot about instruction and presenting a strong image as a principal. When she spoke, she never looked like she had any doubt about what she was going to say. I learned a lot about instructional leadership from her, but not too much about the importance of equity and inclusion.

During the fellowship I was able to glean some important lessons about school leadership, largely through interviewing and observing five principals. While some really understood students, others really only understood adults. I spent a week with each of them, which allowed me to understand the cultures of their schools. I became a believer that leaders create the culture, which largely contributes to a school's successes and failures. I became a believer that leaders create the culture, which largely contributes to a school's successes and failures.

When I graduated, I began applying for school principal positions in the district, but I couldn't get one. During the fellowship, the district paid you the same salary you were receiving in your previous job. In return, you owed three years of principalship in Boston after graduation. They had invested in me and wanted something in return. The best I could find was an assistant principalship at a school in Roxbury. During the two years I spent there, I learned a lot about instructional leadership, but I was told that my stance on racial equity was off-putting to some districts.

HOLDEN MIDDLE SCHOOL

After my second year fulfilling my post-fellowship commitment, I was granted release from my obligation. Three districts showed strong interest in me, but Holden Middle School—located in a small urban city south of Boston—really resonated. I'd grown up nearby, and they already had a reference letter singing my praises from one of my mentors from the Fellows Program. The superintendent, who was midway in his tenure, liked me, and the new deputy superintendent, also Black, was an old acquaintance.

Twenty or so teachers, parents, staff, and school committee members interviewed me. Things seemed to click, and I was offered the school principal position. I had been the only Black candidate and was the first Black principal in the district. There was not a single other faculty member of color at the school.

Within the first three months, various Holden newspapers published articles on me, complete with pictures. Being a man of color, I think, was something that people were curious about. I knew I had to be intentional with everything I did. All eyes were on me, and I had to control the outcomes.

BUILDING A CULTURE OF DIVERSITY

The first thing I did as school principal was write a letter to every faculty member. It said something to the effect of, "Hi, I'm Manuel J. Fernandez, your new principal. A little bit about me. I went to UMass Dartmouth, grew up on the south shore, and was raised in the African American tradition."

I used the letter as an invitation for faculty members to come meet with me in person. I included a questionnaire, shared with me by another Boston Public Schools principal fellow, for them to complete and return to me. First: What works here? Second: What needs improvement? Third: What is the worst thing I could do as your new principal? Fourth: How are decisions regarding your role in this school being made? Forty or so faculty members agreed to come in, and what became clear was that the majority felt that discipline was an overarching issue.

I invited them to help me build a culture that would both address their concerns and sustain what was working well. While I felt the school lacked diversity training, some people thought the diversity situation at the school was positive.. I overheard one teacher refer to every Latina girl referred to as Maria and every Latino boy as José. I was appalled. Early on, I received some hate mail telling me to "Go back to Boston," which I felt was an upgrade from when it used to be "Go back to Africa." People frequently mistook me for the new Black deputy superintendent, despite him being considerably shorter and heavier than I was. He and

I became very close allies. It was a change for the district; they weren't used to having two Black men in leadership positions.

I got a lot of support from my assistant principal; he was my biggest cheerleader. It said a lot, because he had gone for the principal position and hadn't been considered. He knew the school and the district, as he'd grown up in Holden and had been there for years. He was really able to help me understand where people's minds were on everything.

I knew that I had to be strategic with the things I would be putting forward. Any changes needed to be gradual. My entry plan was really about getting to know the school and the people there. If I did it over again, I would have spent more time talking with parents and students.

The middle school was in the high school building, so I spent a lot of time with the high school principal over the first few months. I found him to be very instrumental; he had charisma and taught me about my school and the community. It was evident that many of Holden's Black and Latino kids didn't do well in high school; most of them flunked or were pushed out because of disciplinary issues. We had to do something differently. Although I couldn't do anything for the kids coming out of other middle schools, I could certainly support the kids at Holden. I spent December break gathering data and putting together a PowerPoint presentation on our school's diversity. The first day after break, I sent out an email: "Today, we are having a faculty meeting; we'll be discussing the diversity of our students and achievement, discipline and special education referrals ." Sadly, when educators aren't used to talking about race, the very mention of it is considered somehow racist. The hubbub that day was that I was going to use the meeting to call the faculty racist.

I posed questions, "Has anything about me indicated that I'm a person who would bring you all together as a group to call you racists? Have I done anything to suggest that I would treat you with such disrespect?" That lifted some of the tension, and I started pulling out some facts. I pointed out that a significant percentage of the students of color graduating from our school went on to either flunk high school or not make it to college or vocational school. We were going to deal with these issues using real data in a systematic way, and I invited them to be a part of the process. I also encouraged them to begin having authentic conversations about race and culture. I offered to spend time before or after school meeting with people who wanted to look at a video or read an article or something like that, to get the conversation going.

I had two small groups of teachers and administrators, about four on Tuesdays and 12 on Wednesdays, who would come in to discuss race and culture. The superintendent asked me to do a couple of anti-bias workshops for administrators, and after some racially charged incidents occurred in the district, the Professional Development Committee asked me to do more anti-bias training. Before I knew it, I was training people all over the district.

I was building capacity and putting in measures to ensure that the anti-bias work would continue after I left—and it still does. I created the first formal instructional leadership team in the district. It represented all the disciplines, at every grade level. We met regularly to address ways we could change our instructional practices and raise student achievement. Over time, it's been integrated into the teachers' work each day. They're looking at their curriculum, pedagogical style, and what kids are responding to. They're addressing the needs of the various learning styles represented in each classroom.

TRANSPARENCY

During my first month, I explained to the faculty what I meant when I called myself transparent: "I mean that if you have a problem, you should come and see me. I will do what I can to respond to it—no need to make it the teachers' room topic of the month." I began to value being accessible to all, not just to my leadership team and closest allies. My doors were always open. Every student or teacher could come in without an appointment and say, "You really screwed up today. I'm pissed at you." Or "I don't agree with where we're going on this." Students know if they really wanted to see me, they just tell their teacher, "I need to see Mr. Fernandez"—and they did.

At one point, a Holden teacher approached me, saying that teachers were in the cafeteria talking about me. I grabbed a lunch tray and had a seat at their table and said, "Hey, y'all been talking about me? Don't get upset. I told you when I first got here, if you do not agree with something

I do, then come and see me. I'll keep you informed, and you will have plenty of opportunities to speak your mind. But I guarantee we will have problems if you're talking about me without telling me." People began to trust me; they understood what I meant about being transparent.

MODELING ACCOUNTABILITY

One of the most significant events of my tenure took place during year 3. Our eighth-grade class was the most challenging class of students I've ever met. They were unbelievable. They'd walk around the halls shouting "F this and F that". One day, they were being particularly disruptive during a community meeting. I went in there to talk to them. When I finally got their attention, I said, "You've only got a few more months. You've got to go on to high school, and I can't see how you're going to make it with this kind of attitude. You can't walk around the halls saying "F." They started laughing. I realized my error immediately. "It's not funny," I said. "I shouldn't have tried to quote anybody, and I apologize."

I knew I had made a mistake. I called the superintendent. "Don't worry about it," he assured me. "It'll blow over." I told him it wouldn't and that one of the eighth-grade mothers was already angry with me over something else. I warned him that she was a very formidable adversary and guaranteed him she'd be in touch. My brother happened to be dating a woman who lived in the community. He relayed to me what she had told him: "Some lady in the PTO said you cursed out the kids and told them to go F themselves."

So the next morning at 8:00, my phone rang. It was the superintendent: "Were there any adults in that community meeting besides you?" I gave him the names of the teachers who had been there. After interviewing each of them, he came back to me, "It's just as you said. You didn't swear at them, you quoted them." He said I shouldn't have and asked, "What are we going to do?" I asked him to suspend me, so he told me not to come in on Monday. "No," I replied, "Here's what you need to understand." I explained that when a kid says "F," we suspend them for a day; for a teacher, it would be three days. I had said "F" in front of 100 middle school students and 20 faculty members, so as the highest-ranking official in the building, I should be suspended for a week. "Without pay?" he asked, "Because that's what will happen." I'd have to live with that. I wrote three letters that day addressing the parents, faculty, and students. Then I went away for a week.

When people learned that I had asked to be suspended, I got some emails from teachers and parents saying things like, "You made a mistake; it's not the end of the world. A week's suspension is too harsh." It was a turning point for me in terms of recognizing that it had been a tough year. I hadn't been intentionally immoral, I'd been reactionary, which is the worst thing for a principal to be. When you're reactionary, you lose control of the outcome. By suspending myself, I was able to retroactively take back some of the control of the outcome.

Fast-forward three years. Most of the kids at the high school know me because of the equity work I did annually for World Language Week. The Honor Society there voted me to be the keynote speaker at their induction ceremony. After the induction, a mother and father approached me. "I'm so proud that my daughter's going to be in the Honor Society next year," said the father. "I want to thank you for being the role model that you were for her when she was in middle school. Suspending yourself for swearing made such a difference. My daughter wrote her essay for the Honor Society on that."

DISCIPLINE AND ACHIEVEMENT

Earlier in my career, I had developed a system to determine which students would be allowed which privileges. Holden had a similar program, which I refined. Every week, based on a student's behavior and academics, they would be categorized. If they were "Independent," they received all the rights and privileges afforded a middle school student. Students categorized as "Transitional" were somewhere in the middle. Those whose behavior and academics were even more wanting were designated as "Supervised." They were restricted; they couldn't go to the restroom alone or attend school dances.

The Holden faculty thought the system was wonderful, but I began looking at the numbers. Most of the "Supervised" kids were brown and Black, while the majority of "Independent" kids were white. It was problematic for me. What was worse was that some teachers looked for students who they thought would misbehave and threatened them, "I'm going to get you!" The program didn't work, and I regretted initiating it. We did away with it my last year at Holden.

Overall student achievement slowly improved, but not as much for the groups I was most concerned about: Black, brown, low-income, and students with IEPs. I think that if I had stayed longer, we could have done better. There had been a lot of challenges, many of them systemic, extending beyond the school. We didn't have a solid plan as a school or as a district for how to really challenge the gap. I don't like using the phrase "closing the achievement gap." I prefer to call it "challenging the gap" because it speaks to the various dimensions of the gap between those who have and those who have not. There's the access gap: Who has access to what resources? Who has computers at home? Who has a library at home? Who has adult caregivers who bring them certain academic wisdom and insights before sending them off to school? There's the association gap: Who has friends? Who has mentors? In retrospect, I regret not challenging the academic gap more fiercely.

LEAVING HOLDEN

I had been friendly with the superintendent in Cambridge for many years. When I ran into him at a statewide professional development meeting, he let me know that he was making some changes in Cambridge. He would be changing from a K–8 to a K–5 system and opening four new middle schools. He asked if I was interested in a position. I joked, "No, I *like* driving the hour-plus to and from Holden through the tunnel twice a day." When they put out the announcement for the head of school for Cambridge Street Upper School, he encouraged me to apply.

Leaving Holden was really hard. I felt supported by my faculty, fellow principals, and for the most part, by central administration. I felt supported by my students and parents. I think I was well liked and respected, and I knew that the superintendent was proud of the gains the school had made under my leadership.

During one of my last interviews, the superintendent asked why I wanted to come to Cambridge. I replied; "Because you understand the work I believe in—equity and inclusion. You're a white man who cares. To have a white male superintendent get this, I couldn't ask for a better opportunity." I got the job, but before signing I made it clear: "Your social justice mantra is important to me. I'm not going to pussyfoot around with this. We're going full steam ahead." He said, "That's why I hired you."

THE PRINCIPAL'S PLATFORM

Graduate school taught me that every effective principal needs a platform. Mine has always been social justice, and I'm transparent about that. Even before I was a principal, I believed in equity for everybody. A lot has to do with my own experiences growing up and not being comfortable in school in a mostly white, working-class community. I stood out being the only Black kid at the school, but I was also easily forgotten. Nobody saw my intellectual potential. Everything I had ever been told about myself was that I was intellectually inferior to white folks.

Every kid who comes into a school I lead should be happy to get up in the morning and come to the building and to these teachers, because they know that they're going to be treated well; that they will feel good and be affirmed. I can't guarantee that's going to happen all day, every day, but I can guarantee that we are going to work towards that daily.

There's a sense of urgency for me around this work, around supporting every student. We have so many students who are imperiled every day because of economics, race, mental health, and social-emotional issues. Every day, they need to leave us knowing more than they came with. We need to equip them with the skills they need to pursue their own learning, even when they're not with us. It wasn't about coming to school and shutting it off at 3:00.

THE BIG QUESTION

Through the summer prior to my first year, I hired teachers, a guidance counselor, and an assistant principal. There was one question I asked every candidate, regardless of the position they were applying for: "How has race and culture affected your life and how will that inform your work with our students?" I remember asking one candidate who responded; "I can't really tell you how it's affected my life in a way that sounds impressive, I can only tell you that I know it has, I know I have a lot of work to do, and I hope that if I get this job that you'll help me pursue that work." An honest answer; she got the job. There's only one wrong answer, which is, "It hasn't affected me at all."

ENTRY INTO CAMBRIDGE STREET UPPER SCHOOL

Landing at Cambridge Street Upper School was like landing in nirvana. I had the full support of central administration, support from most of the school committee and a healthy budget. I told my faculty when I first met them, "If you have an issue, you come see me," and they did. Every decision was transparent and involved those affected by it. Very few major decisions were made in the school without me pushing it past the Instructional Leadership Team (ILT) first. I was interested in understanding how a decision might play out: How was this going to play in the faculty room, a team meeting? How was this going to play with kids and families?

The June before the school's grand opening was intense. I was with teachers and administrators constantly, and I was scared shitless. I was responsible for opening a school from top to bottom and for creating a whole new culture. On my first day with my faculty in June, I had them watch a video, *My Brown Eyes*, about a little Korean boy's first day of school. The video showed how students who are different from the norm can be viewed as "less than." Assumptions by school faculty and students about the boy because he was an immigrant led to them treating him with lower expectations. You could see his pain and shame throughout the day. The film also showed how competent and bright the boy was at home.

After watching and discussing it, everybody spent 10 minutes writing one statement explaining what they felt social justice would look like at Cambridge Street Upper School. When we came together in August, we continued with more social justice work. I wanted everyone to acknowledge that as a predominantly white faculty, we had to own our personal and professional racial experiences and the lens we brought to our work. I challenged us to act with intentionality and courage to become culturally proficient educators and meet the needs of our very diverse student body.

From the very beginning, I let it be known that race was an issue we would be dealing with consistently. We were not going to play like it didn't exist, like it didn't matter. It would be difficult at times, but we were going to talk about it. Since then, the entire district has taken steps toward cultural proficiency.

Cultural Proficiency Seminars

To continue professional development around social justice, all faculty members were required to attend weekly 45-minute cultural proficiency meetings, which were initially led by me. I came to realize that being a Black man addressing a predominantly white faculty about a topic as fraught as race hindered honest and fruitful discussion that was required for meaningful change. The solution was to allow teachers to be guided by their peers. Over a dozen faculty members, the majority of whom were white, facilitated these meetings. According to teachers, the shift led to more productive discussions, although the conversations remained difficult—voices cracked, faces flushed, and tears were not uncommon.

All students attended a weekly cultural proficiency seminar as well. We made videos of our students to be used in the seminars, some of which featured Black students sharing about what it's like to be a Black boy here. We showed it to some teachers, and they pointed to one kid and said, "Ah, he's such a little pain." I said, "That's not one of our norms. We listen to people and believe their stories." I pointed out that if the video was from another school, they wouldn't respond that way. They would say, "Those teachers aren't doing the Black kids right!"

During one schoolwide seminar, I showed a video of white kids in this school talking about race and how they saw bias by their teachers against kids of color. One girl hit it right on the head: "I don't think the teachers even know they're doing this. But I think it's important that they know that we see it."

RESPECTING NON-BINARY STUDENTS

I got an email from a student saying, "Mr. Fernandez, I know we have a 'no hat' policy, but I'm asking for permission to wear my hat. The reason I want to wear my hat is because I'm 'non-binary.'" I didn't know what that meant, so I looked it up. The student didn't relate to either gender. They don't see themselves as a male or a female. So they asked if they could wear a hat, and I responded that I would love to talk with them more about it. I wanted to hear more from them, to learn and understand more about their experience. Knowing how much it took for them to do this, I told them they could bring whomever they wanted to the meeting for support. So three people came into my office. At the time, I viewed them as girls. They told me that they are all "theys," and would like to be allowed to wear hats. How could I refuse them the option of wearing a hat if it would make them feel more comfortable engaging in school? I'd already made my decision.

It was a Friday, and I told them they could start wearing hats on Tuesday. I figured I would use Monday to tell the faculty. "What are you going to tell the other students about why we can wear hats?" they asked. I told them that starting that Tuesday, everyone would be allowed to wear hats. This was one of the times where I didn't seek faculty input, this decision was 100 percent my own. I never ask my faculty for permission, but I believe in collaborative leadership; I don't give up all the power, but I believe in giving people pieces of the pie to control. Every once in a while, I take that piece of pie back and I say, "That's not working. You wanted to try it, and I supported you for a year. We aren't doing that anymore."

Two things about the hat situation kept bouncing around my head. First, I grew up in a time when you took off your hat when you walked into a room, especially if you sat down at a table. So when I go out to eat and I see men wearing hats, I'm reminded that I'm from a different generation and have to accept it. Second, I started my career working with urban students. Wearing a hat could mean gang affiliation. What I had to do was assess all the reasons why I didn't like hats in school. I may not have liked the look of the kids wearing their hats crazily, but as long as they weren't obscene, they were allowed to wear them. Now, as my hairline has continued to recede and I have reluctantly embraced my baldness, I wear hats often—especially the school hats.

Eliminating Reading Logs

We did away with weekly reading logs that same year. They weren't helpful, and I had kids missing field trips and receiving poor grades for failing to complete them. I sat down with some teachers and asked them to explain how the logs worked. Four nights a week, students were expected to write two or three lines about what they had read. They explained that on Fridays, teachers would take the logs home to read. With around 100 students each, I simply didn't believe that teachers were reading nearly 400 reading log entries each weekend. It was meaningless compliance. We replaced the system with one-page reflection papers due each Friday.

Shortly after deciding on this shift, we held a special community meeting and asked each student to bring a book. I was on stage in a rocking chair, reading a book. They came in and didn't know what the hell to do. Then, finally they picked up: "Oh he wants us to read a book." So for 15 minutes, my entire school sat in the auditorium, dropped everything, and read. I explained that just because I eliminated the reading logs didn't mean I wanted them to stop reading. I went on, "I'm reading four books right now. Two for work, one 'cause I love history, and the fourth is some mystery that puts me to sleep at night. I am who I am today, ladies and gentlemen, because I read. I grew up in a very poor household, but I traveled all around the world every day without leaving the library. My mother would call the library each evening, and I would hear the ringing and know it must be time for me to go home for dinner."

Respecting Arts and Athletics

We had the strongest arts and athletics programs in the district. Why? Because we made them a priority. We called them the five A's—Arts, Academics, Athletics, Access Wellness, and Association—and they became integrated into students' daily schedules. We allowed kids out of their regular academic classes on a weekly basis just as long as they keep up with their academic work. They missed a different class each time they went to an arts class or practice. If they didn't keep up with their classroom work, then we dealt with it.

My fellow middle school principals and I introduced an athletics program that I proposed that's quite different from other districts. Every kid got to try out and play on any team they were interested in: basketball, volleyball, cross-country, or soccer. Everybody got to play for the whole season, and then two weeks before the season ended, we selected the all-stars and sent them off to a two-week competition with other schools.

HETEROGENEOUS CLASSROOMS

We had heterogeneous mathematics in the seventh grade last year, which meant every seventh-grade class had students from each academic level of performance. Prior to that, the sixth-grade scholars took an assessment that would determine if they were in an accelerated level or a slower-paced math course. It resulted in two cohorts that were 95 percent white and two cohorts that were 95 percent students of color and students on IEP's. It was counter to our belief on equity and inclusion in all aspects of school life. We had to fight for it and were the only school to do it. There was resistance, but our superintendent supported us. Our test run ended up being successful. Currently, every seventh and eighth grade in the district has heterogeneous math.

THE YEAR OF RECALIBRATION

One year, I busted my leg during a winter break snowstorm and couldn't go back to school for four months, until the following April. It was painful to see what the school looked like when I returned. Certain people had taken advantage of gaps in the system, but I blamed myself because the school was supposed to be capable of functioning with the changing of the guard. It was my fault that it wasn't.

Although my leadership is transparent and most of my faculty find me accessible, I have a strong personality. No one is confused as to who is in charge. I listen and consider input from others, but when I make a decision, it is final. In my absence, the administrators in charge did not garner the respect of some faculty members because they were not viewed as strong and as resolute as I am. I've learned from that and now when members of my leadership team are challenged, I don't jump in as I did in the past. Now I work with them to consider what they value, find space for collaboration, and then encourage them to assert themselves so that even when others disagree with them, their decisions are respected and accepted.

When I came back from medical leave, I met with some of the teacher representatives and the union faculty advisor committee. Apparently, folks weren't happy with the way the school had been operating in my absence. They didn't take responsibility for their own work, blaming other people for things that were going on. I guess folks just dropped the ball and said, "Well, I'm not going to do anything because you're not doing anything. Why should I tell people to be quiet in the hallways if you're not going to tell people?"

At the next faculty meeting, I said, "It's been shared with me that folks are really unhappy with the way things have been, so open your laptops and please complete the nine-question survey. I need feedback to understand what has gone on since I've been gone and what we need to do now." Before they left, I had them send me three available dates when they could meet with me for a 30-minute one-on-one session.

The survey asked questions a former colleague shared with me such as: "What works here?" "What needs improvement?" "What is your contribution to what isn't working?" "What are you willing to do to get things to work?" After reading their comments, I had a pretty good idea of what had happened and where we needed to go. I asked only one question during my one-on-one meeting; "How's your year been?" For 30 minutes, they would just tell me about their year. Their views were not nearly as bad as what the faculty representatives had presented to me. One person even said, "I'm having the best year I ever had." But they all agreed that they could see the turmoil with kids who were acting out and folks not being able to maintain order with certain classes.

I identified a number of prevailing themes: (1) student identity, (2) how do we see our students (3) discipline, (4) team collegiality and respect, (5) the relationship between special educators and general educators, (6) the relationship between special education, arts, health, PE, and world language teachers, and (7) the social-emotional issues our kids were facing.

I created task forces around these issues and invited any and every faculty member to serve. I would even pay them to join. Forty of my 62 faculty members volunteered to join and offered recommendations to the task forces. The task force held three retreats where we started picking away at the recommendations. The faculty responded well and appreciated the opportunity to come together with colleagues to address these recommendations.

One of the other things I did wasn't as well received as the task forces and the one-on-one meetings. I changed some teachers' positions. My primary reason was that I believed that sixth grade was the most important grade in middle school. If you didn't get it right in grade 6, you ended up having three years of drama and you'd be ineffective in creating the culture that needs to be embedded if students are going to be successful intellectually, socially, and culturally. I formed the strongest sixth-grade team possible: people who were good educators, classroom managers, and collaborators. That hadn't always been the case with any team.

When making these changes, I tried to be respectful of each individual. I had to let the person know about the change before announcing it to the rest of the faculty. Generally, people wouldn't like what they heard; that they would be losing a partner on their team or that they would have to work with a different grade level. They'd leave that conversation telling people, "You won't *believe* what he did!"

Once each individual had been notified, I shared the new team blueprints with the entire faculty. One person came to me and said, "This is brilliant." Because they could see all the pieces together rather than isolated conversations happening about who was being moved to where. Despite the initial turmoil, I have no regrets about the staffing decisions I made that year.

It had been a year of recalibration. Another change was a shift in how we thought about our students. We had always referred to them as "scholars," but we never clearly defined what a scholar was. I had intentional discussions with faculty about what it meant to be a scholar at our school. It was about more than about simply doing your job; it was about passion and pursuing a vision of what CSUS should be. If a faculty member was there to do the bare minimum, the school wasn't the right place for them. We needed to accentuate the attributes of a scholar, and we began holding monthly schoolwide student-facilitated assemblies to highlight the attributes: social justice, curiosity, honor, originality, leadership, academic excellence, and resilience.

REFLECTIONS

I grew up in the '60s and '70s, and I think because I understood race and the limitations placed upon us as Black males, I was harder on Black male students. At the time, I justified it because I wanted the best for them. I knew the world was going to be more difficult for them, and I wanted them to be prepared; to be strong. But I could have done it differently.

I've gotten older and learned from wiser people who have informed my thinking. I've learned to convey skills and lessons to students in a way that's firm and direct but not harsh. The deepest regret of my career is not trying harder to demonstrate a gentleness, a warmness, when a student—especially a boy—was in a tough place. I could have held them to a higher standard, while showing them I cared by dealing with their issues more gently. Instead I tended to pound my fist and be a tough guy all the time. That's what I was taught, and sometimes it had its place. But for the most part, I think if I had to do it all over again, I would do it a lot differently regarding how I interacted with students who were going down the wrong path.

Recently, I went to the 30th reunion for one of the classes I had advised. They invited me and a few other teachers to come back. My former students were all over me. Mostly white students were there—now as grown adults 48 or 49 years old. They told me, "Oh, you were so wonderful! The way you did this and that!" There was a Black guy there, and he had some nice things to say. But he also said; "You know, we didn't see him the same way you all saw him. You saw him as the funny Black guy from the city who came out to work with the METCO students, but also worked with white students, but we saw him as a strict, very tough disciplinarian." That stuck with me. I'm not saying that I didn't need to be strident and so on, but I think that as I work with young Black and Latino men today who are imperiled, there's a way of getting the point across and still showing respect for the dignity of the person you're talking to.

I think too many times I, and others like me, cross the line when we discipline these kids instead of trying to figure out the root cause. Every behavior has a purpose. There's a reason why students act the way they do. It's taken me a while to learn that, but I've learned it. Hopefully, it shows with the work that I do now.

I'm not in a big hurry to leave. CSUS had been a state designated Level 1 school since its grand opening in 2012. I'm having fun, and I know I'm making a difference in the lives of students, teachers, and parents. When teachers approach me saying "Hey boss, I'm glad I'm at this school!" I know they're not blowing smoke because it takes a lot for them to say that to me. I've been blessed with the ability to select the right people to work in this building and to serve as leaders here.

You have got to build relationships and I will say that I'm not always the best at that with everybody. I have a hard time building relationships with people who don't talk, people who are very reticent and laid back. Recently, I had a teacher ask to speak with me. She told me in so many words, "I feel like you don't like me. You don't appreciate me." She was in tears. It broke my heart. She seemed relieved after our conversation. A couple of days later, she thanked me for allowing her to talk so candidly to me. The fact that she could say that to me is one thing. The fact that I didn't recognize that I wasn't acknowledging her enough is another thing. That conversation informed my thinking.

I remember another situation with one of my best teachers, who also struggled with relationships. Although she was an excellent teacher, the way she talked to people pissed them off. She felt like I wasn't engaging her as much as other teachers; like I had dropped her as a mentee. She approached me and said, "I look up to you and I've made mistakes." Then she hit me where it hurt: "You gave up on me." We spent a lot of time unpeeling what had gotten in our way. I like to think that as a result of our conversation, we are closer now.

There are a lot of things I'm good at as a principal:like I'm a very reliable person. But I have been blind to the fact that there were teachers who needed more from me than I was giving them. I've learned that I need to do a better job of expressing my appreciation for others. In recent years, I've made it a priority to meet one-on-one with each faculty member annually. I make it clear that it's not an assessment, but a conversation. I share about myself but also check in with them. I ask how they are doing; what's working for them; how I can be helpful; and for any other insights they might have. It's meaningful relationship building.

A major goal throughout my career has been to prepare the next generation of teachers of color. There is a sense of urgency in terms of what I'm trying to achieve, because I'm not going to be doing this much longer. I want to cultivate our teachers of color to be skilled and socially conscious teachers. There's a dire need for educators of color, but they are going to be judged more critically. As the rare principal of color, I have an obligation to mentor them warmly and critically.

In the past two years, we have significantly increased the number of people of color on the faculty. They make it a point to interact with me regularly because they view me as the rare mentor of color in their brief career. They are young, energetic, and creative. They are not shy about expressing how they feel about their racial interactions with white faculty or what they observe as the troublesome relationships that some white teachers have with students of color. Many of them have challenged the belief that all the white faculty members operate with a culturally proficient lens. Some have even asked to be excused from the cultural proficiency seminar. That was not something that I was comfortable doing. What I did do was create opportunities for faculty of color and biracial faculty members to meet regularly in affinity groups. White faculty also meet in small affinity groups. Affinity groups have helped the adult community work more intentionally on race-related matters for the benefit of all of our scholars.

Another goal of mine has been to make sure students understand the importance of writing their own stories. I would check in with them: "What's your story?" "Are you writing it, or is it being written for you?" "How can I support you along the way?"

I avoided being a school principal for many, many years. I wish I had learned earlier that I enjoy it and that I'm pretty good at it, because I would have pursued it sooner. The sense of urgency is always there for me. I'm not going to back down from anything or anyone around my values, around social justice for all, equity and inclusion for all, until I retire. Then I'll try to do something else related to that.

LEADERSHIP IN THE ERA OF COVID

Covid19 forced us to transition to remote learning in less than 18 hours. We were alerted via a district-wide email on a Thursday night in March, 2020 that in-person learning would be suspended the next day until further notice. That night the leadership team identified how many scholars were served through free and reduced meals and partnered with food services to provide five days of meals for scholars to bring home at the close of school on Friday. That morning the technology team programmed laptops with virtual meeting capability and provided each scholar a laptop as they left the building. Food services would set up daily distribution sites (including our school) and provide breakfast and lunch to any family

On Monday, we held a virtual community meeting for each grade level to begin building a virtual community, share protocols for online learning, and provide a weekly schedule of classes and events. In addition, teacher assistants and support staff were reassigned to the role of Wellness liaisons to monitor student engagement and intervene with scholars that were not logging on to classes and grade-level events.

We provided a detailed weekly newsletter for the entire school community and held monthly family caregiver listening sessions to build community and to center familial concerns that needed attention.

Our typical in-person advisory groups of 20-25 scholars and 3-4 adults were divided into smaller groups of 5-7 students with one advisor and were renamed Cobra Dens after our school mascot. Dens met three times a week and provided community-building activities and wellness check-ins. It was a model that successfully maintained meaningful connections with scholars, and many other schools in the district adopted it.

Our Scholar Success Team met weekly to review and respond to concerns shared by Wellness Liaisons regarding academic engagement and social isolation. The response included online mental health support and one-on-one tutoring. In addition, through our Family Engagement Team, response teams were tasked with providing gift cards for families experiencing food insecurity as well as internet hotspots.

Adults: both educators and family caregivers were putting up a strong front for students, but they also were experiencing social isolation and uncertainty. So we contracted with a community group to provide adult community-building events and trauma healing sessions. In addition, I held weekly virtual office hours for faculty members to drop in with concerns or just to maintain connections.

All educator teams were reconfigured by grade and department, and support staff were assigned to groups to support online community activities and to receive and provide updates on student progress. Also, once every three weeks, teams set up at the school entrance to distribute school supplies and exchange laptops that were inoperable.

After the murder of George Floyd, consistent with our school's active anti-racist initiative we sponsored separate adult and scholar virtual events that were well attended and provided support for all.

With all of its drawbacks, the pandemic tapped into our school's innovative spirit, and we found exciting and more student-centered ways to teach, affirm, and meet the needs of students and adults.

Before applying to be Head of Cambridge Street Upper School (CSUS), Manuel had carefully prepared himself to be a skilled and reflective principal. He grew professionally as he changed positions. He deepened his leadership skills at Xonward Charter School, Boston School's Principal Fellows program and Holden Middle School. He came to CSUS with a well thought out and tested practice that communicated what he stood for and aspired to achieve as a school leader. Social justice and anti-racism (SJAR) were the central elements of his vision. Manuel passionately believed SJAR was what the world needed and he was going to be a missionary for that message. When Manuel articulated his vision to Cambridge's superintendent at the time of his employment, the superintendent endorsed it enthusiastically and suggested that it was influential in his being hired in the district.

Manuel started coalescing the CSUS faculty to higher performance by personally practicing and promulgating social justice and anti-racism and inspiring his faculty to follow his lead. Manuel served as an inspirational leader through his passion for social justice and active anti-racism. As a newly opened middle school, Manuel was in the position to offer faculty a choice in whether they joined the school. His hiring decisions were based on faculty affirmation that SJAR should be an integral part of the school's culture. Manuel used SJAR as the centerpiece of his criteria for selecting teachers and staff. Those who were invested in ongoing learning and internalizing of SJAR were given priority for hiring.

Manuel brought his passion in this area to his leadership, providing safe spaces in which to hold difficult conversations between a leader of color and a predominantly white faculty. The experience prepared faculty to participate in and/or lead seminars advancing SJAR at CSUS and other schools within the Cambridge district. Social justice and anti-racist teaching coalesced CSUS faculty for a common purpose. Enabling teachers to chart their professional learning course by selecting the task force they would join increased faculty commitment to successfully completing the aspiration.

Joining with others in the district, CSUS dismantled the stratified mathematics curriculum; replacing it with heterogeneously grouped learning centers that provided equal opportunity for all students. Their inspiring work was promulgated across the district as CSUS teachers educated their colleagues around topics of social justice and active anti-racism.

While faculty momentum faltered during Manuel's four months absence, it was re-energized upon his return and they responded to the COVID crisis with unity and care for their community. They did so with a determination and passion exemplified by Manuel's model. For his part, Manuel recognized the value of working with his Leadership Team, and sought their input in decision-making.

As Covid-19 raged and public schools had to reinvent education repeatedly in an ever changing landscape, Manuel and his faculty kept the social/emotional well-being of their students at the forefront. He maintained the student advisory groups during the months of virtual-only learning. In addition he held weekly office hours to support faculty. As the racial pandemic unfolded, Manuel's school contracted with a community group to hold sessions for adults devoted to dealing with trauma and building community.

CONCLUSION

COMMON COLLABORATIVE PRACTICES FOR HEIGHTENED STUDENT LEARNING

Each of the six leadership cases highlights the leader's unique decisions and outcomes. This section focuses on the practices that a number of principals in this study utilized to build collaborative cultures that had the promise of increasing student learning. All six schools' cultures were reflections of their leaders' passionate values:

- Mark Nardelli's passionate interest in socio-emotional phenomena precipitated a significant shift in the school's mission and practices.

- Beth Ludwig created a school-based team to assess and plan for students with social/emotional needs, responding to major challenges the classroom teachers faced and building their capacity to support the students in their care.

- Matt Stahl used "having fun" as an attraction for faculty to reconfigure their instruction to be both fun and effective.

- Manuel J. Fernandez articulated his vision for integrating social and racial justice into the school culture.

- Eva Thompson was passionate and optimistic about the capacity of collaborative and skilled teacher teams to make a positive difference in student learning and was successful at that effort.

- Henry Turner focused on distributing leadership to his department heads, empowering them to lead their teams and work collaboratively on behalf of all students.

While each of the six principals brought their unique, distinctive missions to their administrative practices, six common collaborative practices emerged.

1. Building personal relationships: All leaders prioritized developing personal relationships with their faculty with various degrees of intimacy. For example:

- Henry Turner personally modeled building a trusting culture by reaching out to the faculty individually for a relationship of mutual trust, one in which he could comfortably discuss, for example, personal family and race relations.

- Beth Ludwig explicitly worked with the faculty to establish her authentic self. She acted with candor and courage in sharing information about her partner and the impending birth of their baby.

- Matt Stahl made personal relationships a hallmark of his leadership style. He made himself vulnerable and was transparent in his decision-making. By joining his faculty in fun, free time activities and modeling the value of having fun, he was highly successful in transferring that approach to instruction and improved student performance.

2. Creating a sense of urgency: Leaders utilized student data, teacher reports, and observations of faculty interactions to draw attention to a problem faced by the school. Next they posed opportunities to work collaboratively to resolve the issue. By highlighting information and experiences of the faculty, the leader built a sense of urgency focused on a solution. For example:

- Mark Nardelli shared referral data for special education services and encouraged faculty to respond to student needs through teaching positive behaviors and targeting lagging reading skills. By adding trained staff in classrooms during literacy, teachers were better able to meet student needs. His staff significantly lowered the referrals in the building.

- Manuel J. Fernandez communicated the urgency of creating equitable school experiences for all students by seeking teachers who made this work their priority as well. He opened the school year by sharing a video showing inequitable treatment of a newly immigrated student as he started the school year. He wove the topic of social justice into all his actions and communications.

• Beth Ludwig recognized the challenges of educating students who moved frequently, leaving the school with an ever-changing student community. Teachers were challenged to meet the needs of students who had a wide range of learning levels and comfort in school. The BESST Team grew out of the urgency to meet student needs. It provided faculty with the support they needed to develop a safe and caring learning environment.

3. Distributing leadership: All leaders distributed decision making to their faculty for problem solving with the expectations that one: it would give faculty practice in developing their own leadership skills and two: there would be improved problem-solving by staff organizationally closer to the issue at hand. For example:

• Henry Turner prepared his cabinet for more autonomous decision-making by turning meetings over to them. Responding to managerial questions via email enabled Henry to provide meeting time that the Leadership Team could devote to curriculum implementation and student learning.

• Manuel J. Fernandez facilitated training for his faculty in anti-bias and racial justice topics. Subsequently, the faculty members became trainers of their colleagues across the district.

• Eva Thompson facilitated sessions designed to communicate the value of collaborative work with peers. Subsequently, she distributed leadership to her faculty so that they could prioritize aspects of the school for focused work, and select the topic of greatest interest to them to investigate.

4. Prioritizing social-emotional wellbeing of students: Many of the leaders recognized the importance of ensuring that all students felt welcome in the school, that their learning styles, backgrounds and lived experiences were valued, and that their families were part of the community as well. For example:

• Mark Nardelli guided his faculty to create positive experiences for at-risk students whose behavior frequently stood in the way of everyone's learning. Giving these opportunities to lead and receive praise for their positive actions frequently shifted how the students viewed themselves.

• Matt Stahl recognized the potential value of joy in teaching and learning. As teachers brought fun into their classrooms, students became engaged in the learning and motivated to succeed.

5. Expanding pedagogy to engage diverse student population: Multiple principals sought to expand pedagogy in order to engage a diverse student population; provide a range of access points for learners including those whose first language was not English and those with identified special needs; and offer a variety of methods students would use to demonstrate mastery. For example:

• Mark Nardelli implemented a schedule that enabled specialists to join classroom teachers during the literacy block. With more adults in classrooms, all students received targeted instruction and more attention and feedback around their learning. Referrals for special education dropped dramatically as general education teachers differentiated their teaching to effectively match student needs.

• Henry Turner invited students to assist with planning and implementing the rally after Confederate flag incident and the subsequent anti-racist initiatives at the school.

6. Inspiring faculty to extraordinary efforts: A number of leaders inspired staff to deliver extraordinary efforts. As the leaders in the school, they created and articulated opportunities for faculty to choose to participate. Those opportunities required extra effort but held the promise of collaborating with colleagues to solve significant problems facing the school, or to initiate innovative changes. Moreover, the collective effort could be personally uplifting. The possibility of personally experiencing fulfilling outcomes was at the risk of committing to the extra effort with no possible rewards. Faculty made a choice to participate thus heightening their commitment to it. For example:

- Mark Nardelli positioned identifying and working to remediate at-risk students as a unique opportunity for self-fulfillment by making a significant difference in an underserved population of students.

- Matt Stahl supported a coaching model requested by teachers that enables faculty to observe, provide feedback and learn from colleagues working directly with students in real time.

- Eva Thompson facilitated professional development for faculty in order to model how making the extra effort to collaborate positively impacted teachers and students.

In summary, this book provides data-based practices demonstrated by bold school principals, that serve as guidelines for creating schools of heightened student learning.

About the Authors

Gerald C. Leader, lead author (Gerry), is Professor Emeritus of Boston University. He earned an MBA in 1961 and a Doctorate in 1965 from Harvard Graduate School of Business Administration. Following his service as a commanding officer in the U.S. Army, Professor Leader's career history of five decades includes roles as an educator with leadership practice, research and teaching. He has focused on leadership, first in the private sector then in non-profit organizations, government agencies and subsequently in secondary education. In 2002, Professor Leader founded and directed the Educator Leadership Institute (ELI), a Massachusetts state licensed principal preparation program until his retirement in 2012. He is the co-author with Amy Stern of *Real Leaders, Real Schools - Stories of Success Against Enormous Odds* published by Harvard University Press in 2008. Professor Leader lives in Brookline, Massachusetts.

Email: gleader@bu.edu

Louise Lipsitz, collaborating author, served in public and independent schools for over four decades as a classroom teacher, special educator and elementary principal. She worked as a building leader for twenty three years. She received a BS from Franklin and Marshall College in 1974; earned an MEd. in Special Education in 1979 and a Certificate of Advanced Graduate Studies in Educational Leadership in 1998, both from Boston College. Ms. Lipsitz was a faculty member at Educator Leadership Institute from 2006-2008. She has supervised both teacher and principal candidates through Boston College, Simmons College and the Educator Leadership Institute. Ms. Lipsitz lives in Brookline, Massachusetts.

Email: lplipsitz@gmail.com

ACKNOWLEDGMENTS

GERALD C. LEADER, LEAD AUTHOR

This book grew from the real stories of public school principals: Eva Thompson, Matt Stahl, Henry Turner, Beth Ludwig, Mark Nardelli, and Manuel J. Fernandez. These leaders courageously and repeatedly opened their daily lives as educational leaders, allowing others to read about them and learn from their experiences. For the trust they placed in me, I am deeply appreciative.

Louise Lipsitz, my research and writing collaborator, brought acute observational skills and narrative traction that gave life and nuance to the book.

As lead author I owe significant gratitude to my administrative assistants for their commitment, diligence, competence, patience and perseverance: Mori Insinger, Andrea Epstein, Antony Abiawad, Naomi Brown and especially Jonny Rosadino who gave a tremendous final push to the manuscript.

A loving thank you goes to my daughter Kristin who created an arresting cover design that graces our book.

My heartfelt gratitude extends to I. Michael Grossman, author and The EBook Bakery publisher who has generously shepherded our manuscript to publication.

My life partner, Lucy Aptekar, who provided endless hours of conversations about content and subsequent editing collaboration, has relentless belief in me and my ability to produce this book, even when I questioned its feasibility. For this, I will be forever grateful.

As collaborating author I have been honored to work alongside Gerald C. Leader. He demonstrated an unwavering commitment; ensuring that the stories included in this book were told with respect for the school leaders and their faculty members.

Recognizing the common threads across the cases, he highlighted the principals' abilities to coalesce their teacher communities thereby enhancing student learning. I am indebted to Gerald for his invitation to join the project.

The support I received from my soulmate, Lewis Lipsitz, has been unfailing. He encouraged my participation in the collaboration and provided feedback every step of the way.

www.ingramcontent.com/pod-product-compliance
Lightning Source LLC
Chambersburg PA
CBHW050123280326
41933CB00010B/1228